중학 영어

기적의 영문법

1

중학 영어 기적의 영문법 1

저 자 방정인
발행인 고본화
발 행 반석출판사
2020년 3월 5일 초판 1쇄 인쇄
2020년 3월 10일 초판 1쇄 발행
홈페이지 www.bansok.co.kr
이메일 bansok@bansok.co.kr
블로그 blog.naver.com/bansokbooks

07547 서울시 강서구 양천로 583. B동 1007호
(서울시 강서구 염창동 240-21번지 우림블루나인 비즈니스센터 B동 1007호)
대표전화 02) 2093-3399 **팩 스** 02) 2093-3393
출 판 부 02) 2093-3395 **영업부** 02) 2093-3396
등록번호 제315-2008-000033호

ISBN 978-89-7172-912-0 (13740)

중학 영어

기적의
영문법

1

반석출판사
Bansok

머리말

학문의 길은 험난하다. 영어를 잘 하기 위해서는 모든 학문이 그렇듯이 영어에 흥미와 관심을 얼마나 쏟느냐가 중요하다. 영어 공부는 초기에 누구나 흥미를 갖고 대하게 된다. 중학교 1학년 중반이 되면 문법이 서서히 등장하고, 중학교 2학년부터는 복잡한 문법이 나오기 시작한다. 이때가 영어를 공부하는 학생들에게는 아주 중요한 시기이다. 바로 공부하는 학생이 영어에 흥미를 갖느냐 갖지 못하느냐가 결정되기 때문이다.

중학교 3학년 과정을 마친 학생들은 보통 기본영어를 공부하는 것으로 알고 있다. 실은 고등학교 예비생들에게는 기본영어가 너무 어렵다. 이들이 고등학교에 진학하여 영어를 공부하는 데 필요한 수준에 알맞은 영문법 책이 요구된다.

『중학 영어 기적의 영문법』은 누구나 단어에 대한 부담 없이 공부해 나갈 수 있도록 기초 단어 700여 개로 문장을 구성하였고, 문법 내용은 중학교 교과과정부터 고등학교 전 과정의 모든 문법을 다루었다. 그리고 본서는 문법 항목이 나올 때마다 PATTERN PRACTICE(문형 연습)를 많이 수록하여 같은 내용의 문법을 여러 번 되풀이함으로써 그 문법의 항목만큼은 완벽하게 터득하도록 편집되었다. Exercise(연습문제)도 주로 주관식 문제로 구성하였다.

고입·대입을 준비하는 수험생들에게 『중학 영어 기적의 영문법』 1권과 2권으로 영문법만은 총정리 되리라 믿는다.

저자 방정인

4

이 책의 특징 및 활용 방법

❶ '문장'에서부터 '문장 전환'에 이르기까지 중학교 및 고등학교 전 과정에서 다루는 모든 문법 사항들을 설명해 두었습니다. 문장을 이루는 기본 요소에서부터 문장을 어떻게 바꾸는지에 이르기까지 차근차근 공부해 나가다 보면 어느새 영어 문법을 익숙하게 사용하고 있을 것입니다.

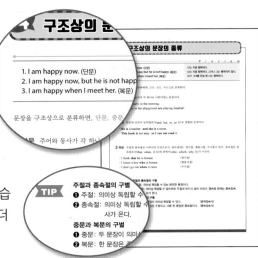

❷ 중요한 개념이나 부가적인 내용들은 TIP에 담았습니다. 문법을 공부하면서 개념이 분명치 않거나 더 궁금했던 사항들은 TIP을 참조하세요.

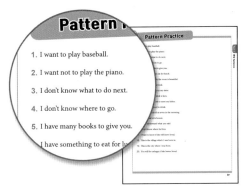

❸ 앞에서 공부한 문법 내용들을 담은 문장들을 Pattern Practice에 따로 모았습니다. 문장들을 읽고 해석해 보면서 공부한 내용들을 상기해 보세요.

❹ 해석, 영작, 지시대로 바꾸기, 알맞은 말을 써 넣기 등을 통해 공부한 문법 사항을 잘 습득했는지 확인해 보세요. 한 호흡마다 있는 연습문제들로 문법 사항의 습득 여부를 쉽게 확인할 수 있습니다.

연습문제

1. 다음 영문을 우리말로 옮기시오.
   (1) My brother watches the sheep.
   (2) I bought a pair of glasses.
   (3) I met a poet and a teacher.
   (4) I met a poet and teacher.
   (5) He goes to his uncle's.

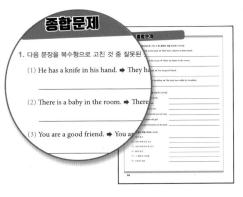

❺ 단원에서 학습한 내용을 종합적으로 확인하는 종합문제를 통해서 보다 자유롭게 영어 문법을 사용할 수 있게 됩니다.

목차

중학 영어
기적의 영문법 1

Part 1

문장

SENTENCE

8품사

1. **Tom** is a **student**. (명사)
2. **He** is a student. (대명사)
3. I **go** to school. (동사)
4. He is a **good** student. (형용사)
5. He is a **very** good student. (부사)
6. She goes **to** school **at** seven. (전치사)
7. She **and** I are good friends. (접속사)
8. **Oh**, how kind she is! (감탄사)

톰은 학생이다.
그는 학생이다.
나는 학교에 간다.
그는 훌륭한 학생이다.
그는 매우 훌륭한 학생이다.
그녀는 7시에 학교에 간다.
그녀와 나는 좋은 친구들이다.
오, 그녀는 참 친절하구나!

문장을 구성하고 있는 각 단어는 그 의미와 구실에 따라 8가지로 나눌 수 있다. 이를 8품사라고 한다.

1 명사(Noun) ·················· 사람이나 사물의 이름을 나타내는 말이다.
Tom, student, book, school 등

2 대명사(Pronoun) ········ 명사 대신에 쓰이는 말이다.
I, you, he, this, that 등

3 동사(Verb) ·················· 사람과 사물의 동작이나 상태를 나타내는 말이다.
am, are, is, play, study 등

4 형용사(Adjective) ········ 명사나 대명사를 수식하는 말이다.
good, pretty, kind, little 등

5 부사(Adverb) ··············· 동사, 형용사 또는 다른 부사를 수식하는 말이다.
very, well, early 등

6 전치사(preposition) ··· 명사 또는 대명사 앞에 놓여서 다른 단어와의 관계를 나타내는 말로서, 형용사구 또는 부사구를 만든다.
in, at, of, to 등

7 접속사(Conjunction) ··· 단어와 단어, 구와 구, 절과 절을 연결하는 말이다.
and, but, or, that, if 등

8 감탄사(Interjection) ··· 기쁨, 슬픔, 놀람 등의 여러 가지 감정을 나타내는 말이다.
oh, ah 등

문장의 요소와 5형식

P·r·e·v·i·e·w

1. I go to school. (1형식)	나는 학교에 간다.
2. I am a student. (2형식)	나는 학생이다.
3. I have a book. (3형식)	나는 책을 가지고 있다.
4. I gave him a book. (4형식)	나는 그에게 책을 주었다.
5. I call him Tom. (5형식)	나는 그를 톰이라고 부른다.

1 문장의 4요소 문장은 주어, 동사, 목적어, 보어라는 4가지 중요한 요소로 뼈대를 이루는데 이를 문장의 4요소라고 한다.

1 주어(~은, ~는, ~이, ~가) 주부의 중심이 되는 말로 명사, 대명사, 명사 상당어구
2 동사(~하다, ~이다) 술부의 중심이 되는 말로 주어를 설명하는 말
3 목적어(~을, ~에게) 동사의 동작을 받는 말로 명사, 대명사, 명사 상당어구
4 보어 주어와 목적어를 설명·보충하는 말로 명사, 대명사, 형용사 또는 그 상당어구

TIP

8품사와 문장의 4요소 구별
❶ 8품사: 문장을 이루는 단어들의 각 갈래
❷ 4요소: 각 갈래들이 문장 속에서 하는 역할

2 동사의 종류

• **자동사**: 목적어가 필요 없는 동사로 완전자동사, 불완전자동사
• **타동사**: 목적어가 필요한 동사로 완전타동사, 수여동사, 불완전타동사

1 완전자동사 보어가 필요 없는 동사		(1형식 동사)
2 불완전자동사 보어(주격보어)가 필요한 동사		(2형식 동사)
3 완전타동사 목적어만 필요한 동사		(3형식 동사)
4 수여동사 목적어가 2개(간접목적어, 직접목적어) 필요한 동사		(4형식 동사)
5 불완전타동사 목적어와 보어(목적격보어)가 필요한 동사		(5형식 동사)

3 문장의 5형식

[1형식] **주어 + 동사(S + V)** ~이 있다, ~은 ~한다 | 주어와 동사만으로 완전한 뜻을 나타낸다.

· Birds fly.
· Birds fly in the sky.

① 완전자동사: fly, go, come, be(am, are, is) 등
② 주어가 될 수 있는 품사: 명사, 대명사, 명사 상당어구

[2형식] **주어 + 동사 + 보어(S + V + C)** ~이다, ~이 되다 | 주어와 동사만으로 완전한 뜻을 나타낼 수 없으므로 보충하는 말, 즉 보어가 필요하다.

· She is a doctor.
· She is happy.

① 불완전자동사: be(am, are, is), become, look, smell 등
② 보어로 쓰이는 품사: 명사, 대명사, 형용사 그리고 그 상당어구
③ 명사 상당어구: 부정사, 동명사, 명사구, 명사절 등 4가지
④ 형용사 역할을 하는 것들: 부정사, 현재분사, 과거분사, 형용사구, 형용사절 등 5가지
⑤ 불완전자동사는 be동사로 바꾸어도 뜻이 통한다.

ex. He became a doctor. ≒ He was a doctor.
She looks happy. ≒ She is happy.

⑥ be동사는 '~있다(존재)'로 해석되면 완전자동사로 1형식 동사이고, '~이다(서술)'로 해석되면 불완전자동사로 2형식 동사이다.

· He is at home. ·········· (1형식)
· He is a student. ······ (2형식)

[3형식] **주어 + 동사 + 목적어(S + V + O)** ~을 ~한다 | 목적어 하나만을 필요로 하는 동사, 즉 완전타동사이다.

· He likes me.
· I read a book.

① 목적어로 쓰이는 것들: 명사, 대명사, 부정사, 동명사, 명사구, 명사절 등
② 완전타동사: like, want, read, have 등

[4형식] **주어 + 동사 + 간접목적어 + 직접목적어(S + V + IO + DO)** ~에게 ~을 해 준다

· I gave her a book. = I gave a book to her.
· I made him a box. = I made a box for him.

① 수여동사: give, send, show, make, buy, cook, ask 등
② 간접목적어: 주로 사람이나 동물이 온다. (~에게)로 해석한다.
③ 직접목적어: 주로 사물이 온다. (~를, ~을)로 해석한다.

④ 4형식에서 간접목적어와 직접목적어의 위치를 바꾸면 3형식이 된다. 이때 간접목적어 앞에 to, for, of를 써 넣는다.

> • give ~ to   • send ~ to   • show ~ to
> • teach ~ to   • make ~ for   • buy ~ for
> • cook ~ for   • ask ~ of
> ※ make ~ for, buy ~ for, cook ~ for, ask ~ of 등을 제외한 대부분의 수여동사는 ~to 로 한다.

5형식 **주어 + 동사 + 목적어 + 보어(S + V + O + C)** ~을 ~라고 한다 | 목적어를 설명하여 동사의 의미를 보충하는 말 즉, 목적격 보어가 필요하다. 목적어와 목적격보어의 사이에는 의미상 〈주어 + 동사〉의 관계가 성립된다.

• I made him a teacher.
• I made him happy.
• I want him to go home.
• I made him go home.
• I saw him going home.
• I saw him punished by his mother.

① 불완전타동사: make, call, think, want, see, hear 등
② 목적격보어가 되는 것들: 명사, 대명사, 형용사, to부정사, 원형부정사, 현재분사, 과거분사 등 7가지가 있다.

4형식과 5형식의 구별
4형식은 IO≠DO의 관계가 성립되고, 5형식은 O=C의 관계가 성립된다.

• I made her a box. (her≠a box)   4형식
• I made her a teacher. (her=a teacher)   5형식
• I promised her to go there. (her≠to go)   4형식
• I wanted her to go there. (her=to go)   5형식

Pattern Practice

1. I go.

2. I go to school.

3. I go to school at seven.

4. I go to school at seven in the morning.

5. There is a book on the desk.

6. He is at home.

7. He is a student.

8. He is happy.

9. She looks happy.

10. I want them.

11. I want a book.

12. I want to read a book.

13. I enjoy reading a book.

14. I don't know what to do.

15. I think that he is busy.

16. I gave him a book. (= I gave a book to him.)

17. He teaches us English. (= He teaches English to us.)

18. He made me a small house. (= He made a small house for me.)

19. He bought me a car. (= He bought a car for me.)

20. She asked me a question. (= She asked a question of me.)

21. She promised me to go home.

22. She asked me to go home.

23. She told me to go to school.

24. I made him a doctor.

25. I made him sad.

26. I want him to go to school.

27. I made him go to school.

28. I saw him go to school.

29. I saw him going to school.

30. I saw him punished by his mother.

연습문제

1. 다음 문장의 형식을 쓰고 우리말로 옮기시오.

(1) He goes to school by bus.　　　(　) _____

(2) He made a teacher.　　　　　　(　) _____

(3) He made a house.　　　　　　　(　) _____

(4) He made me a house.　　　　　 (　) _____

(5) She made me a teacher.　　　　 (　) _____

(6) She got up early yesterday.　　　(　) _____

(7) She made me happy.　　　　　　(　) _____

(8) She bought a book for me.　　　 (　) _____

(9) She wants to meet me.　　　　　(　) _____

(10) He wants me to meet her.　　　 (　) _____

(11) He saw me read a book.　　　　(　) _____

(12) He saw me reading a book.　　　(　) _____

(13) He gave me some books.　　　　(　) _____

(14) She enjoys reading a book.　　　(　) _____

(15) She thinks that he is wise.　　　(　) _____

(16) She doesn't know what to do.　　(　) _____

(17) She heard me sing a song.　　　 (　) _____

(18) She made me sing a song.　　　 (　) _____

(19) There are some books in it.　　　(　) _____

(20) He became a scientist.　　　　　(　) _____

2. 다음 문장을 영작하시오.

(1) 나는 어제 집에 있었다. _____

(2) 나는 의사였다. _____

(3) 나는 아침 일찍 일어난다. _____

(4) 나는 그녀가 공부하기를 원한다. _____

(5) 나는 그녀가 공부하는 것을 보았다. _____

(6) 나는 그녀가 공부하고 있는 것을 보았다. _____

(7) 나는 무엇을 해야 할지 모른다. _____

(8) 나는 그가 정직하다는 것을 안다. _____

(9) 나는 그에게 상자를 만들어주었다. _____

(10) 나는 그를 의사로 만들었다. _____

용법상의 문장의 종류

1. I am a student. / I am not a student. (평서문)	나는 학생이다. / 나는 학생이 아니다.
2. Are you a student? / Yes, I am. (의문사가 없는 의문문)	당신은 학생입니까? / 예, 그렇습니다.
Where are you? / I am at home. (의문사가 있는 의문문)	당신은 어디에 있습니까? / 나는 집에 있습니다.
Is this an apple or an orange? (선택의문문)	이것은 사과입니까 혹은 오렌지입니까?
/ It is an apple.	/그것은 사과입니다.
You are happy, aren't you? (부가의문문)	당신은 행복합니다, 그렇지 않아요?
Do you know who he is? (간접의문문)	당신은 그가 누구인지 압니까?
3. Go home. / Don't go home. (명령문)	집에 가라. / 집에 가지 말아라.
Let's go home. / Let's not go home. (명령문)	집에 가자. / 집에 가지 말자.
4. How pretty she is! (감탄문)	그녀는 참 예쁘구나!
What a pretty girl she is! (감탄문)	그녀는 참 예쁜 여자네!

1 평서문 사실 그대로 진술하는 글이다. 평서문에는 긍정문(~이다)과 부정문(~이 아니다)이 있다.

부정문 만드는 방법

❶ **be동사의 부정문**: be동사 바로 뒤에 not을 써 넣는다.
  · I am a student. ➡ I am not a student.
  · You are a student. ➡ You are not a student.
  · He is a student. ➡ He is not a student.

❷ **have동사의 부정문**: have동사 바로 앞에 don't, doesn't를 써 넣는다. 이때 has를 have(동사원형)로
  바꾼다.
  · I have a book. ➡ I don't have a book.
  · You have a book. ➡ You don't have a book.
  · She has a book. ➡ She doesn't have a book.

  ☐ **don't**: have가 올 때 즉, 주어가 1인칭, 2인칭 및 모든 복수일 때
  ☐ **doesn't**: has가 올 때 즉, 주어가 3인칭 단수일 때

❸ **일반동사의 부정문**: have동사의 부정문과 같다.
  · I go to school. ➡ I don't go to school.
  · You go to school. ➡ You don't go to school.
  · She goes to school. ➡ She doesn't go to school.

  ☐ **don't**: 주어가 1인칭, 2인칭 및 모든 복수일 때
  ☐ **doesn't**: 주어가 3인칭 단수일 때

TIP

1인칭: 말하는 사람, 즉 I(단수), we(복수)

2인칭: 그 말을 듣는 사람, 즉 you(단수), you(복수)

3인칭: 1인칭과 2인칭을 제외한 세상의 모든 것, 즉 he, she, this, desk 등

❹ **조동사의 부정문:** be동사의 부정문과 같다.

· I can speak English. ➡ I can not speak English.

· You can speak English. ➡ You can not speak English.

· He can speak English. ➡ He can not speak English.

2 의문문 의문을 나타내는 글로 의문사 없는 의문문, 의문사 있는 의문문, 선택의문문, 부가의문문, 간접 의문문 등이 있다.

의문문 만드는 방법

❶ **be동사의 의문문:** 주어와 be동사의 위치를 서로 바꾼다.

· I am a student. ➡ Am I a student?

· You are a student. ➡ Are you a student?

· He is a student. ➡ Is he a student?

❷ **have동사의 의문문:** 주어 앞에 Do나 Does를 써 넣는다.

· I have a book. ➡ Do I have a book?

· You have a book. ➡ Do you have a book?

· She has a book. ➡ Does she have a book?

☐ **Do:** have동사가 올 때, 즉 주어가 1인칭, 2인칭 및 모든 복수일 때

☐ **Does:** has가 올 때, 즉 주어가 3인칭 단수이고, 시제가 현재일 때

❸ **일반동사의 의문문:** have동사의 의문문과 같다.

· I go to school. ➡ Do I go to school?

· You go to school. ➡ Do you go to school?

· She goes to school. ➡ Does she go to school?

❹ **조동사의 의문문:** be동사의 의문문과 같다.

· I can speak English. ➡ Can I speak English?

· You can speak English. ➡ Can you speak English?

· He can speak English. ➡ Can he speak English?

Pattern Practice

1. I **am** a good student.

2. You **are** a good student.

3. He **is** a good student.

4. I **was** a good student.

5. You **were** a good student.

6. He **was** a good student.

7. There **is** a piano in the room.

8. There **are** some flowers in the living room.

9. There **was** a piano in the room.

10. There **were** some flowers in the living room.

11. I **have** a good friend.

12. You **have** a good friend.

13. He **has** a good friend.

14. I **had** a good friend, too.

15. You **had** a good friend, too.

16. He **had** a good friend, too.

17. I **go** to school.

18. You **go** home.

19. She **goes** to the market.

20. I **went** to school.

21. You **went** home.

22. She **went** to the market.

23. I **play** baseball.

24. I **can** play baseball.

25. He **plays** baseball.

26. He **can** play baseball.

27. You **played** baseball.

28. You **could** play baseball.

29. She **is able to** speak Korean.

30. She **has to** stay here.

연습문제

1. 다음 문장을 부정문으로 고치시오.

(1) I am a good student. _____

(2) You are a good student. _____

(3) He is a good student. _____

(4) There is a book on the desk. _____

(5) I have a good friend. _____

(6) You have a good friend. _____

(7) She has a good friend. _____

(8) She goes to school, too. _____

(9) She went to school, too. _____

(10) She had some friends, too. _____

(11) He plays baseball. _____

(12) He can play baseball. _____

(13) He is able to play baseball. _____

(14) He wanted to go to school. _____

(15) He has to study hard. _____

2. 다음 문장을 의문문으로 고치시오.

(1) I am a good student. _____

(2) My sister is beautiful. _____

(3) My sisters are beautiful. _____

(4) There was a book on the desk, too. _____

(5) He is reading a book. _____

(6) He reads a book. _____

(7) He has some flowers. _____

(8) He has to stay here. _____

(9) He had some flowers. _____

(10) He goes to church. _____

(11) He went to church. _____

(12) She plays tennis well, too. _____

(13) She can play tennis well, too. _____

(14) She is able to play tennis well, too. _____

(15) She wants to go to church. _____

1 **의문사 없는 의문문**   Yes나 No로 대답하는 의문문으로 끝을 올려 읽는다.

  · Are you a student? ➡ Yes, I am. (a student.) / No, I am not. (a student.)
  · Can you speak English? ➡ Yes, I can. / No, I can't.

  · Is there a book on the desk? ➡ Yes, there is. / No, there isn't.
  · Do you have a book? ➡ Yes, I do. / No, I don't.

  · Does he go to school? ➡ Yes, he does. / No, he doesn't.
  · Did she go to school? ➡ Yes, she did. / No, she didn't.

2 **의문사 있는 의문문**   의문사가 항상 앞에 나오고 Yes나 No로 대답하지 않으며 끝을 내려 읽는다. 의문사
                    자신이 주어일 때는 〈의문사 주어 + 동사〉의 어순이고, 의문사 자신이 주어가 아닐
                    때는 〈의문사 + be동사(조동사) + 주어〉의 어순이다.

  · Who are you? ➡ I am Tom.
  · Who likes you? ➡ He likes me.

  · Whom do you like? ➡ I like him.
  · When do you start? ➡ I start at seven.

  · Where does she live? ➡ She lives in Seoul.
  · How did she go? ➡ She went by bus.

3 **선택의문문**   둘 중에서 하나를 선택하는 의문문으로 Yes나 No로 대답하지 않으며, 보통 or 앞은 올려 읽
              고 끝은 내려 읽는다.

  · Is this a book or a notebook? ➡ It is a book.
  · Do you like an orange or an apple? ➡ I like an apple.
  · Which do you like better, spring or autumn? ➡ I like autumn better than spring.

Pattern Practice

1. Am I a teacher?
   Yes. (Sir. / Ma'am)
   Yes, you are.
   Yes, you're a teacher.
   Yes, you are a teacher.

   Am I a teacher?
   No. (Sir. / Ma'am.)
   No, you aren't. You are a doctor.
   No, you're not. You are a doctor.
   No, you are not a teacher.

2. Are you a doctor?
   Yes. (Sir. / Ma'am.)
   Yes, I am.
   Yes, I'm a doctor.
   Yes, I am a doctor.

   Are you a doctor?
   No. (Sir. / Ma'am.)
   No, I'm not. I'm a teacher.
   No, I'm not a doctor. I'm a teacher.
   No, I am not a doctor. I am a teacher.

3. Is Mr. Brown a farmer?
   Yes. (Sir. / Ma'am.)
   Yes, he is.
   Yes, he's a farmer.
   Yes, he is a farmer.

   Is Mr. Brown a farmer?
   No. (Sir. / Ma'am.)
   No, he's not. He's a doctor.
   No, he isn't. He's a doctor.
   No, he isn't a farmer. He's a doctor.

4. Do you have a book?
   Yes. (Sir. / Ma'am.)
   Yes, I do.
   Yes, I've a book.
   Yes, I have a book.

   Do you have a book?
   No. (Sir. / Ma'am.)
   No, I don't. I have a pen.
   No, I don't have a book. I've a pen.
   No, I do not have a book. I've a pen.

5. Does Miss Brown have a car?
   Yes. (Sir. / Ma'am.)
   Yes, she does.
   Yes, she has a car.

   Does Miss Brown have a car?
   No. (Sir. / Ma'am.)
   No, she doesn't. She has a truck.
   No, she doesn't have one. She has a truck.

6. Does he go to school?
   Yes. (Sir. / Ma'am.)
   Yes, he does.
   Yes, he goes to school.

   Does he go to school?
   No. (Sir. / Ma'am.)
   No, he doesn't. He goes home.
   No, he doesn't go to school.

7. Did you go to school?
   Yes. (Sir. / Ma'am.)
   Yes, I did.
   Yes, I went to school.

   Did you go to school?
   No. (Sir. / Ma'am.)
   No, I didn't.
   No, I didn't go to school. I went home.

8. Can you speak English?
   Yes. (Sir. / Ma'am.)
   Yes, I can.
   Yes, I can speak English.

   Can you speak English?
   No. (Sir. / Ma'am.)
   No, I can't. I can speak French.
   No, I cannot speak English.

다음 ( ) 안에 알맞은 낱말을 써 넣으시오.

(1) Are you a doctor?

Yes, ( ) ( ).

Yes, ( ) ( ) ( ).

Yes, ( ) ( ) ( ) ( ).

(2) Are you a nurse?

No, ( ) ( ).

No, ( ) ( ) ( ) ( ). ( ) a doctor.

(3) Is your father a farmer?

Yes, ( ) ( ).

Yes, ( ) ( ) ( ).

Yes, ( ) ( ) ( ) ( ).

(4) Is your mother a doctor?

No, ( ) ( ).

No, ( ) ( ) ( ) ( ). ( ) a nurse.

No, ( ) ( ) ( ) ( ) ( ). ( ) a nurse.

(5) Is there a book on the desk?

Yes, ( ) ( ).

Yes, ( ) ( ) ( ) ( ) on the desk.

(6) Are there any books on the desk?

No, ( ) ( ) ( ).

No, ( ) ( ) ( ) books on the desk.

(7) Do you have a book?

Yes, ( ) ( ).

Yes, ( ) ( ) ( ) ( ).

(8) Do they have many books?

No, ( ) ( ).

No, ( ) ( ) ( ) ( ) ( ).

(9) Does she go to school?

Yes, ( ) ( ).

Yes, ( ) ( ) ( ) ( ).

(10) Did he go to school?

No, ( ) ( ).

No, ( ) ( ) ( ) ( ) ( ).

(11) Can you speak English?

Yes, ( ) ( ).

Yes, ( ) ( ) ( ) ( ).

Pattern Practice

1. **Who** are you?

   I am **Tom**. / I am **her brother**.

2. **What** are you?

   I am **a student**. / I am **a teacher**.

3. **What time** is it?

   It is **seven thirty**. / It is **half past seven**.

4. **What day** is it today?

   It is **Sunday** today.

5. **What's the date** today?

   It's **September 16**.

6. **When** is your birthday?

   My birthday is **March 27**.

7. **When** does she start?

   She starts **at six** in the morning.

8. **Where** do you live?

   I live **in Seoul**.

9. **Why** were you absent yesterday?

   Because I was sick.

10. **How** did you go to school?

    I went to school **by bus**.

11. Is she **a doctor or a nurse**?

    She is **a doctor**.

12. Is he **a doctor or a teacher**?

    He is **a teacher**.

13. Which do you like **better**, swimming or skating?

    I like swimming **better than** skating.

14. Which do you like **better**, this one or that one?

    I like this one **better than** that one.

15. Which do you like **best**, spring, summer, autumn or winter?

    I like summer **best of all**.

다음 (　) 안에 알맞은 낱말을 써 넣으시오.

(1) (　　) are you?

I am Tom.

(2) (　　) are you?

I am a doctor.

(3) (　　) is Miss Brown?

She is my sister.

(4) What (　　) is it?

It is seven thirty.

(5) What (　　) is it today?

It is Sunday today.

(6) What's (　　) (　　) today?

It's March 27.

(7) What (　　) does she start?

She starts at seven.

(8) (　　) does she start?

She starts at seven.

(9) (　　) is your birthday?

My birthday is September 16.

(10) (　　) do you live?

I live in Seoul.

(11) (　　) were you absent yesterday?

Because I was sick.

(12) (　　) did you go to school?

I went to school by bus.

(13) (　　) loved me?

Mr. Brown did.

(14) (　　) do you want?

I want a story book.

4 **부가의문문** 평서문 뒤에 짧게 덧붙인 의문문으로, 상대방에게 다짐을 하거나 동의를 구할 때 쓰이는 구어체이다. 보통 긍정문 뒤에는 부정의문문, 부정문 뒤에는 긍정의문문이 온다. 명령문 뒤에도 부가의문문이 온다.

• She is pretty, isn't she? 그녀는 예쁘지요, 그렇지 않아요?
• You don't know my name, do you? 제 이름을 모르시지요, 그렇지요?

부가의문문 만드는 방법

❶ **평서문의 부가의문문**: 주 문장이 긍정이면 부가의문문은 부정의문문이다. 주 문장이 부정이면 부가의문문은 긍정의문문이다. 부가의문문의 주어는 본 문장의 주어가 남자이면 he, 여자이면 she, 사물이면 it, 복수면 they로 한다. 부가의문문이 부정의문문일 때 반드시 줄인 말을 쓴다.

• He is happy, isn't he?
• He is not happy, is he?

• He has a book, doesn't he?
• He doesn't have a book, does he?

• The boys read many books, don't they?
• The girls didn't read many books, did they?

• Mary can speak Korean, can't she?
• Tom cannot speak Korean, can he?

❷ **명령문의 부가의문문**: 직접명령문에는 항상 will you?로 쓴다. 간접명령문 Let's가 오면 shall we?로 한다.

• Go to school, will you?
• Don't go to school, will you?

• Let's go to school, shall we?
• Let's not go to school, shall we?

부가의문문 읽는 법
상대방의 동의를 구할 때는 끝을 내려 읽고, 상대방에게 자기 말을 확인하고자 할 때는 끝을 올려 읽는다.
• You are happy, aren't you?   Yes, I am.   (동의)
• It is fine, isn't it?   Yes, it is.   (확인)
　　　　　　　　　　　　　　　No, it isn't.   (확인)

Pattern Practice

1. You are happy, **aren't you**?

2. You are not happy, **are you**?

3. It is fine today, **isn't it**?

4. It is not fine today, **is it**?

5. The lady is beautiful, **isn't she**?

6. The lady isn't beautiful, **is she**?

7. The man is handsome, **isn't he**?

8. The man isn't handsome, **is he**?

9. This book is interesting, **isn't it**?

10. These books are interesting, **aren't they**?

11. She can speak Korean well, **can't she**?

12. You will read this book, **won't you**?

13. You will not read this book, **will you**?

14. Go home quickly, **will you**?

15. Don't go home quickly, **will you**?

16. Let's go to school, **shall we**?

17. Let's not go to school, **shall we**?

18. You know his name, **don't you**?

19. You don't know his name, **do you**?

20. You went to school, **didn't you**?

21. You didn't go to school, **did you**?

22. Tom has many books, **doesn't he**?

23. Tom doesn't have many books, **does he**?

24. Jane had many books, **didn't she**?

25. Jane didn't have many books, **did she**?

26. Tom is reading a book, **isn't he**?

27. Tom is not reading a book, **is he**?

28. Tom has seen a elephant, **hasn't he**?

29. Tom has not seen an elephant, **has he**?

30. Jane was loved by his mother, **wasn't she**?

연습문제

1. 다음 밑줄을 친 곳에 알맞은 부가의문문을 써 넣으시오.

(1) You are happy, _____?

(2) You are not happy, _____?

(3) You buy a car, _____?

(4) You don't buy a car, _____?

(5) You can speak Korean, _____?

(6) You can't speak Korean, _____?

(7) You will read many books in the library, _____?

(8) You will not read many books in the library, _____?

(9) It is fine today, _____?

(10) It is not fine today, _____?

(11) He is a kind teacher, _____?

(12) He is not a good teacher, _____?

(13) She speaks English well, _____?

(14) She doesn't speak English well, _____?

(15) Tom went home quickly, _____?

(16) Jane went home quickly, _____?

(17) The boy has many books, _____?

(18) The girl doesn't have many books, _____?

(19) The boy has to study hard, _____?

(20) The boy has seen a tiger, _____?

(21) Go to school, _____?

(22) Don't go to school, _____?

(23) Let's go to school, _____?

(24) Let's not go to school, _____?

(25) He was reading a book, _____?

연습문제

2. 다음 문장을 영작하시오.

(1) 그녀는 행복하지요? (그녀는 행복합니다, 그렇지 않아요?)

_____

(2) 오늘은 날씨가 좋지요? (오늘은 날씨가 좋습니다, 그렇지 않아요?)

_____

(3) 당신 피곤하지요? (당신은 피곤합니다, 그렇지 않아요?)

_____

(4) 당신은 아프지 않죠?

_____

(5) 당신은 졸리지요?

_____

5 간접의문문 의문사로 시작되는 의문문이 다른 글의 일부가 되어 절을 이룰 때 이를 간접의문문이라 한다.

간접의문문의 어순은 〈의문사 + 주어 + 동사〉이고 명사절이다.

- Who is he? 그는 누구입니까?   (직접의문문)
- I don't know who he is. 나는 그가 누구인지 모른다.   (간접의문문)

간접의문문 만드는 방법

- Do you know? + Who is he?
  ➡ Do you know who he is?

- Do you think? + Who is he?
  ➡ Who do you think he is?

❶ **〈의문사 + 주어 + 동사〉의 어순**: 의문사가 있을 때에는 그 의문사를 그대로 쓰고, 의문사가 없을 때에는 if나 whether를 써서 두 문장을 연결한다.

- I don't know. + Who is she?
  ➡ I don't know who she is.

- I don't know. + Is she honest?
  ➡ I don't know if she is honest.

- I don't know. + Where does he live?
  ➡ I don't know where he lives.

- I don't know. + When did he go?
  ➡ I don't know when he went.

❷ **〈의문사 + do you think + 주어 + 동사〉의 어순**: think, believe, say, guess, suppose 등의 동사가 쓰일 때에는 의문사가 문장의 맨 앞에 놓인다.

- Do you think? + Who is he?
  ➡ Who do you think he is?

- Do you think? + Who was he?
  ➡ Who do you think he was?

- Do you believe? + What does he study?
  ➡ What do you believe he studies?

- Do you believe? + What did he study?
  ➡ What do you believe he studied?

3 명령문 명령, 의뢰, 금지 등을 나타내는 말로서 주어를 생략한다.

명령문 만드는 방법

❶ **직접명령문(2인칭명령문):** 주어를 생략하고 원형동사를 쓴다.

· You study hard. ➡ Study hard.

· You don't study hard. ➡ Don't study hard.

· You are kind. ➡ Be kind.

· You are not kind. ➡ Don't be kind.

❷ **간접명령문(1, 3인칭명령문):** 주어를 생략하고 〈Let + 목적어 + 원형동사〉의 형식을 취한다.

· I go home. ➡ Let me go home.

· He goes home. ➡ Let him go home.

· We go home. ➡ Let us go home.

· We go home. ➡ Let's go home.

· We don't go home. ➡ Let's not go home.

4 감탄문 강한 감정을 나타내는 문장으로 How나 What으로 시작하고 끝에 감탄 부호(!)를 붙인다.

1 〈How + 형용사(부사) + 주어 + 동사!〉

· How pretty this girl is! ➡ This girl is very pretty.

2 〈What + (a, an) + 형용사 + 명사 + 주어 + 동사!〉

· What a pretty girl this is! ➡ This is a very pretty girl.

감탄문 만드는 방법

❶ **How가 문두에 오는 감탄문**

This girl is very pretty.

형용사 뒤에 명사가 없으면 How를 쓴다. very 자리에 How를 써서 문두에 놓고 〈주어 + 동사〉의 어순으로 뒤에 놓는다.

This girl is / very pretty.

How

How pretty this girl is!

❷ **What이 문두에 오는 감탄문**

This is a very pretty girl.

형용사 뒤에 명사가 있으면 What을 쓴다. very 자리에 What을 써서 문두에 놓고 〈주어 + 동사〉의 어순으로 뒤에 놓는다.

This is / a very pretty girl.

What

What a pretty girl this is!

Pattern Practice

1. Do you know who she is?

2. Do you know who she was?

3. Who do you think she is?

4. Who do you think she was?

5. I don't know when he will buy a car.

6. I don't know when he bought a car.

7. Do you know where he studies English?

8. Do you know where he studied English?

9. Where do you believe he studies English?

10. Where do you believe he studied English?

11. Read many books.

12. Don't read many books.

13. Let us read many books.

14. Let us not read many books.

15. Let's read many books.

16. Let's not read many books.

17. Be good to your friends.

18. Don't be bad to your friends.

19. Let him go right now.

20. Don't let him go right now.

21. How beautiful you are!

22. What a beautiful girl you are!

23. You are very beautiful.

24. You are a very beautiful girl.

25. This flower is very beautiful.

26. How beautiful this flower is!

27. This is a very beautiful flower.

28. What a beautiful flower this is!

29. He runs very fast.

30. How fast he runs!

1. 다음 두 문장을 연결하여 간접의문문으로 만드시오.

(1) Do you know?

　　Who is she?　　　_____

(2) Do you think?

　　Who is he?　　　_____

(3) Do you know?

　　Who likes you?　　_____

(4) Do you think?

　　Who likes you?　　_____

(5) Do you know?

　　Who loved you?　　_____

(6) Do you think?

　　Who loved you?　　_____

(7) Do you know?

　　Where does he live?　　_____

(8) Do you think?

　　Where does he live?　　_____

(9) Do you know?

　　When did she start?　　_____

(10) Do you think?

　　When did she start?　　_____

2. 다음 문장을 명령문으로 만드시오.

(1) You go home quickly. _____

(2) You don't go home quickly. _____

(3) You are kind to him. _____

(4) I know his name. _____

(5) He knows my name. _____

3. 다음 문장을 감탄문으로 만드시오.

(1) She is very beautiful. _____

(2) She is a very beautiful girl. _____

(3) This house is very nice. _____

(4) This is a very nice house. _____

(5) The rabbit runs very fast. _____

구조상의 문장의 종류

1. I am happy now. (단문)   나는 지금 행복하다.
2. I am happy now, but he is not happy. (중문)   나는 지금 행복하다. 그러나 그는 행복하지 않다.
3. I am happy when I meet her. (복문)   내가 그녀를 만날 때 나는 행복하다.

문장을 구조상으로 분류하면, 단문, 중문, 복문으로 분류된다.

1 단문 주어와 동사가 각 하나로 이루어지는 문장이다.

- **I get up** early in the morning.
- **The boys** in the playground **are** playing baseball.

2 중문 단문과 단문이 등위접속사(and, but, or, so 등)로 결합된 문장이다.

- **He is** a teacher, **and she is** a nurse.
- **This book is** not easy, **so I can not read** it.

3 복문 주절과 종속절로 이루어진 문장으로서, 종속절에는 명사절, 형용사절, 부사절이 있다. 종속절은 종속접속사(that, when, if 등)와 관계사(who, which, why 등)가 이끈다.

- I think **that** he is honest.   (명사절)
- I know a boy **who** is honest.   (형용사절)
- I don't go out **when** it rains.   (부사절)

주절과 종속절의 구별
❶ 주절: 의미상 독립할 수 있는 완전한 문장이다.
❷ 종속절: 의미상 독립할 수 없으므로 주절과 반드시 같이 쓰인다. 종속절 앞에는 종속접속사가 온다.

중문과 복문의 구별
❶ 중문: 두 문장이 의미상 독립할 수 있다.   (등위접속사)
❷ 복문: 한 문장은 주절이고, 다른 한 문장은 종속절이다.   (종속접속사)

Chapter

05 구와 절

P·r·e·v·i·e·w

1. **To study English** is not easy. (명사구)	영어를 공부하는 것은 쉽지 않다.
2. The book **on the desk** is mine. (형용사구)	책상 위에 있는 책은 나의 것이다.
3. There is a book **on the desk**. (부사구)	책상 위에 책이 있다.
4. I don't know when he will start. (명사절)	나는 그가 언제 떠날지 모른다.
5. I know the day when he was born. (형용사절)	나는 그가 태어난 날을 안다.
6. I am happy when I meet her. (부사절)	내가 그녀를 만날 때 나는 행복하다.

1 구의 종류 구는 두 개 이상의 단어가 모여서 품사와 같은 구실을 한다. 구는 주어와 동사를 갖추지 못한 어군이다. 구에는 명사구, 형용사구, 부사구가 있다.

1 명사구 명사처럼 주어, 목적어, 보어로 쓰인다. 부정사(to + 동사원형)가 명사구로 쓰인다.

- **To study English** is not easy.   (주어)
- I want **to study English**.   (목적어)
- My hope is **to study English**.   (보어)

2 형용사구 형용사처럼 명사를 수식하거나 보어로 쓰인다. 부정사, 분사, 〈전치사 + 명사〉 등이 형용사 구로 쓰인다. 명사를 수식할 때는 명사 바로 뒤에서 수식한다.

- I have something **to tell you**.   (부정사)
- I know a man **reading a book**.   (분사)
- The man **in the room** is my father.   (전치사 + 명사)

3 부사구 부사처럼 동사, 형용사, 부사를 수식한다. 부정사, 〈전치사 + 명사〉 등이 부사구로 쓰인다. 부정사 용법에서 부사적 용법은 모두 부사구에 속하며, 분사구문도 모두 부사구에 속한다.

- English is not easy **to learn**.   (부정사)
- I go **to school at seven**.   (전치사 + 명사)

2 절의 종류 절은 주어와 동사를 갖춘 완전한 문장이다. 절은 하나의 품사와 같은 구실을 한다. 절(종속 절)에는 명사절, 형용사절, 부사절이 있다.

■1 명사절 명사처럼 주어, 목적어, 보어로 쓰인다. 명사절은 접속사 that과 if(whether), 관계대명사 what, 간접의문문의 의문사로 유도된다.

- I think **that she is busy**.　　　　　　　(접속사 that)
- I don't know **if she is happy**.　　　　　(접속사 if)
- I don't know **what he said**.　　　　　　(관계대명사 what)
- I don't know **when he went home**.　　　(의문사 when)

■2 형용사절 형용사처럼 명사, 대명사를 수식한다. 관계대명사와 관계부사로 유도되며 반드시 명사와 대 명사 뒤에 온다.

- This is the man **who teaches us English**.　　(관계대명사)
- This is the house **where he lives**.　　　　　(관계부사)

■3 부사절 부사처럼 동사, 형용사, 부사를 수식한다. 종속접속사(when, where, because, if, though 등)로 유도되는 절이다.

- I was absent yesterday **because I was sick**. (종속접속사)
- **If it is fine today**, we will go on a picnic.　(종속접속사)
- **Though he is poor**, he is happy.　　　　　(종속접속사)

Pattern Practice

1. I want to play baseball.

2. I want not to play the piano.

3. I don't know what to do next.

4. I don't know where to go.

5. I have many books to give you.

6. I have something to eat for lunch.

7. The baby sleeping in the room is beautiful.

8. I saw him reading a book.

9. The girl in the room is my sister.

10. The book on the desk is hers.

11. I went to New York to meet my father.

12. This water is good to drink.

13. He goes to school at seven in the morning.

14. I think that he is honest.

15. I can't understand what you said.

16. I don't know where he lives.

17. I want to know if she will leave Seoul.

18. This is the village which I was born in.

19. This is the city where I was born.

20. You will be unhappy if she leaves Seoul.

연습문제

1. 다음 ( ) 안에 밑줄 친 구의 종류를 써 넣으시오.

    (1) There is a book <u>on the desk</u>.   (   )

    (2) The book <u>on the desk</u> is mine.   (   )

    (3) My hobby is <u>to read books</u>.   (   )

    (4) I have many books <u>to read</u>.   (   )

    (5) I went <u>to the library</u> <u>to read many books</u>.   (   ) (   )

    (6) I went <u>to New York</u> <u>two days ago</u>.   (   ) (   )

    (7) I got up <u>at six</u> <u>in the morning</u>.   (   ) (   )

    (8) I don't know <u>what to do next</u>.   (   )

    (9) I don't know <u>where to go</u>.   (   )

    (10) Many birds fly <u>in the sky</u>.   (   )

2. 다음 ( ) 안에 밑줄 친 절의 종류를 써 넣으시오.

    (1) I thought <u>that he was honest</u>.   (   )

    (2) This is the first man <u>that he saw</u>.   (   )

    (3) This is the village <u>where he was born</u>. (   )

    (4) I don't know <u>where he was born</u>.   (   )

    (5) I am so busy <u>when I write a book</u>.   (   )

종합문제

1. 다음 문장을 ( ) 안의 지시대로 바꿔 쓰시오.

(1) There are some books on the desk. (의문문)

_____

(2) He went to school at seven. (부정문)

_____

(3) She is very beautiful. (감탄문)

_____

(4) You are kind to others. (명령문)

_____

(5) I don't know. Where does he live? (간접의문문)

_____

2. 다음 ( ) 안에 문장의 형식을 써 넣고 우리말로 옮기시오.

(1) He goes to school by bus. ( ) _____

(2) She made him happy. ( ) _____

(3) Do you know when she will leave Seoul? ( ) _____

(4) She sent me some flowers. ( ) _____

(5) She looks very beautiful. ( ) _____

3. 다음 ( ) 안에 알맞은 말을 써 넣으시오.

(1) It is fine today, ( )?

(2) Mr. Brown teaches us English, ( )?

(3) Study hard in class, ( )?

(4) ( ) a beautiful flower it is!

(5) Did you study English?

No, ( ) ( ). I ( ) Korean.

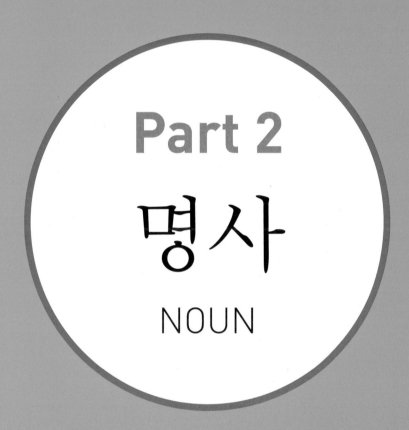

Part 2

명사

NOUN

명사의 종류

P·r·e·v·i·e·w

1. I have many **books** in my **room**. (보통명사)	나는 나의 방에 많은 책을 가지고 있다.
2. **My family** is a large one. (집합명사)	나의 가족은 대가족이다.
3. **Tom** lives in **New York**. (고유명사)	톰은 뉴욕에서 산다.
4. I like **milk** very much. (물질명사)	나는 우유를 매우 좋아한다.
5. **Art** is long, **life** is short. (추상명사)	예술은 길고, 인생은 짧다.

명사는 생물과 사물의 이름을 나타내는 말로 셀 수 있는지 없는지에 따라 셀 수 있는 명사(가산명사)와 셀 수 없는 명사(불가산명사)로 나눈다. 또한 그 나타내는 뜻에 따라 보통명사, 집합명사, 고유명사, 물질명사, 추상명사의 5종류가 있다.

1 셀 수 있는 명사(가산명사) 단수형과 복수형이 있다.

1 보통명사 일정한 모양을 갖고 있는 생물과 사물의 이름이다.

• boy, dog, tree, desk, name 등

일정한 형태는 없어도 단위 구분이 확실한 명사는 보통명사로 취급한다.
• day, week, month, year, hour 등

2 집합명사 사람과 사물의 집합체를 나타내는 말이다.

• family, class, people 등

2 셀 수 없는 명사(불가산명사) 셀 수 없기 때문에 단수와 복수가 없다.

1 고유명사 인명, 지명, 특정한 이름을 나타내는 말이다.

• Mr. Brown, Tom, Seoul, Korea 등

2 물질명사 주로 일정한 형태가 없는 물질을 나타내는 말이다.

• water, coffee, milk, air 등

3 추상명사 눈에 보이지 않는 성질, 상태, 행위 등을 나타내는 말이다.

• peace, happiness, art, life, kindness 등

3 보통명사의 특징과 용법

1 보통명사는 한 개를 나타내는 단수형과 둘 이상을 나타내는 복수형이 있다.

- She has **a book** in her hand.
- She has **two books** in her hand.
- They have **two books** in their hands.

- **The boy** is happy.
- **The boys** are happy.

- There is **a book** on the desk.
- There are **books** on the desk.

2 일정한 형태는 없어도 셀 수 있는 것이면 보통명사로 취급한다.

- I have been ill for **a week**.
- I have been ill for **two weeks**.

3 단수명사 앞에는 관사(a, an, the)를 붙이거나, 관사와 대치할 수 있는 말(this, my, Tom's 등)을 써 넣어야 한다.

- I like **a** car. / I like **this** car.
- I like **an** apple. / I like **that** apple.
- This is **a** book. / This is **my** book.
- **The** book is there. / **My** book is there.

4 **보통명사의 추상명사화**   보통명사 앞에 정관사 the를 붙여 추상적인 의미를 갖는다.

- **The pen** is mightier than **the sword**.
- I found **the artist** in him.

5 **보통명사의 고유명사화**   가족의 이름, 즉 아버지, 어머니, 할아버지 등을 마치 사람 이름처럼 첫 글자를 대문자로 써서 고유명사같이 쓰인다.

- **My mother** wants me to study hard.
- **Mother** wants me to study hard.

- I want to go there with **my father**.
- I want to go there with **Father**.

4 집합명사의 특징과 용법

1 사람이나 사물의 집합체를 나타내는 명사이다.

- My **class** is a large one.
- The Koreans are a diligent **people**.
- The **fleet** is in the harbor.

2 집합명사와 군집명사

① 집합명사: 구성원 전원을 한 집합체로 취급한다. 이때는 단수와 복수가 있다.

- His **family** is not a large one.
- Their **families** are not large ones.

② 군집명사: 집합체를 구성하고 있는 하나하나에 중점을 두어 생각한다. 이때는 비록 단수형이지만 복수의 뜻이 있어 복수 취급을 한다.

- His **family** are all diligent.
- Our **class** are all diligent.

5 고유명사의 특징과 용법

1 사람과 사물(지명)의 고유한 이름으로 쓰이는 명사이다. 첫 글자는 항상 대문자로 쓰고 원칙적으로 관사를 붙이지 않는다.

- **Junho** lives in **Seoul**.
- **Korea** is a beautiful country.

2 사람의 이름, 지명, 요일과 달의 이름, 천체의 이름 등은 고유명사에 속한다.

① 인명: Mary, Chanho, Mr. Brown, Miss Kim 등
② 지명: Korea, America, China, Seoul, London 등
③ 요일과 달: Sunday, Monday, March, Christmas 등
④ 천체: Venus(금성), Mars(화성), Jupiter(목성) 등

▶▶ the sun, the moon, the earth 등은 보통명사로 취급한다.

3 고유명사의 보통명사화

- I want to be **a Newton**. (~와 같은 사람)
- He is **a Mr**. **Brown**. (~라고 하는 사람)
- My father is **a Brown**. (~ 집안사람)

6 물질명사의 특징과 용법

1 물질명사의 종류   고체, 액체, 기체로 된 물질을 나타내는 명사이다.

- sugar, gold, water, milk, air, gas, fruit, chalk, money, bread, butter 등

2 물질명사는 셀 수 없기 때문에 수량을 나타낼 때는 of를 사용한다.

- a cup of coffee   two cups of coffee
- a glass of water   two glasses of water
- a piece of chalk   two pieces of chalk
- a sheet of paper   two sheets of paper
- a cake of soap   two cakes of soap

3 물질명사의 보통명사화   물질의 종류, 제품, 개체를 나타낼 때는 보통명사로 취급하여 단수와 복수가 있다.

- coffee (커피), coffees (커피 종류)
- glass (유리), a glass (유리잔)
- paper (종이), a paper (신문)

7 추상명사의 특징과 용법

1 추상명사의 종류   사람이나 사물의 성질, 상태, 동작을 나타내는 명사이다. 추상명사는 대부분 동사와 형용사에서 만들어진 것이 많다.

- young — youth   • kind — kindness   • happy — happiness
- love — love   • act — action   • live — life

2 추상명사의 보통명사화   추상명사가 구체적인 행위나 종류를 나타낼 때는 보통명사로 단수와 복수형이 있다.

- Thank you for your **kindness**. / She has done me **a kindness**.
- I like her **beauty**. / She is **a beauty**.

3 추상명사의 특별 용법

① of + 추상명사 = 형용사
- He is a man **of wisdom**. = He is a **wise** man.

② with + 추상명사 = 부사
- He can do it **with ease**. = He can do it **easily**.

Pattern Practice

1. My brother is a good student.

2. The Koreans are a diligent people.

3. There are many peoples in Asia.

4. There are many people in the park.

5. Chanho went to America.

6. Would you like some coffee?

7. Happiness is in mind.

8. There are twelve months in a year.

9. A dog is a faithful animal.

10. The dog is a faithful animal.

11. Dogs are faithful animals.

12. I want to go to my uncle's farm.

13. I want to go to Uncle's farm.

14. A Shakespeare cannot be a Newton.

15. A Mr. Brown came to meet you the other day.

16. There are many Kims in our class.

17. Please bring me five sheets of paper.

18. My glasses are made of glass.

19. I am happy because happiness is in my mind.

20. My mother is a beauty.

연습문제

1. 다음 영문을 우리말로 옮기시오.

(1) There is a notebook in the bag. _____

(2) There are some notebooks in the bag. _____

(3) The pen is mightier than the sword. _____

(4) My class is a large one. _____

(5) My class are all diligent. _____

(6) I met a Miss Brown. _____

(7) A Shakespeare cannot be a Newton. _____

(8) I am happy because happiness is in my mind. _____

(9) The dog is a clever animal. _____

(10) There are many people in the park. _____

(11) There are many peoples in Asia. _____

(12) Miss Kim is a beauty. _____

(13) There are many Kims in our class. _____

(14) I bought a pair of glasses. _____

(15) I want to go to my uncle's farm. _____

2. 다음 문장을 영작하시오.

(1) 나는 비누 한 장을 샀다. _____

(2) 나는 뉴턴과 같은 과학자가 되고 싶다. _____

(3) 그는 미국에 가기를 원한다. _____

(4) 나의 가족은 모두 부지런하다. _____

(5) 커피 한 잔 드시겠습니까? _____

3. 다음 ( ) 안에 알맞은 말을 써 넣으시오.

(1) Please bring me a (   ) of milk.

(2) Would you like a (　　　　) of coffee?

(3) Please give me three (　　　　) of chalk.

(4) I bought six (　　　　) of soap.

(5) Will you bring a (　　　　) of paper?

4. 다음 (　) 안에서 알맞은 말을 고르시오.

(1) My family (are, is) a large one.

(2) My family (are, is) all diligent.

(3) Their families (are, is) large ones.

(4) There (are, is) many peoples in Asia.

(5) There (are, is) many people in the park.

5. 다음 문장에서 잘못된 곳을 바르게 고치시오.

(1) I want to go there with father.　＿＿＿＿＿＿＿＿＿＿＿＿

(2) Please give me some waters.　＿＿＿＿＿＿＿＿＿＿＿＿

(3) He is Newton of Korea.　＿＿＿＿＿＿＿＿＿＿＿＿

(4) Mr. Tom is my friend.　＿＿＿＿＿＿＿＿＿＿＿＿

(5) Thank you for your kind.　＿＿＿＿＿＿＿＿＿＿＿＿

6. 다음 밑줄 친 명사의 종류를 써 넣으시오.

(1) I want to be a Newton.　(　　　　　)

(2) Which do you like better, coffee or milk?　(　　　　　)

(3) There are some people in the park.　(　　　　　)

(4) My mother is very happy.　(　　　　　)

(5) Newton is a great scientist.　(　　　　　)

명사의 수

셀 수 있는 명사인 보통명사와 집합명사에는 단수형과 복수형이 있다. 명사의 복수형을 만드는 방법에는 규칙변화와 불규칙변화가 있다.

1 규칙변화 명사의 어미에 -s나 -es를 붙인다.

1 단수형 어미에 -s를 붙인다.

단수	복수	단수	복수
book	books	map	maps
door	doors	boy	boys

2 어미가 s, sh, ch, x로 끝날 때 -es를 붙인다.

단수	복수	단수	복수
bus	buses	brush	brushes
bench	benches	box	boxes

3 〈자음 + o〉로 끝나는 명사는 -es를 붙이고, 〈모음 + o〉로 끝나는 명사는 -s를 붙인다.

단수	복수	단수	복수
hero	heroes	potato	potatoes
zoo	zoos	radio	radios

▶▶ 예외: piano – pianos, photo – photos, solo – solos

4 〈자음 + y〉로 끝나는 명사는 y를 i로 고치고 -es를 붙인다.

단수	복수	단수	복수
baby	babies	lady	ladies

5 〈모음 + y〉로 끝나면 그대로 -s를 붙인다.

단수	복수	단수	복수
boy	boys	key	keys

6 어미가 f, fe로 끝나면 f → v, fe → v로 고치고 -es를 붙인다.

단수	복수	단수	복수
leaf	leaves	knife	knives

▶▶ 예외: roof – roofs, safe – safes

Part 2 명사 Noun

2 불규칙 변화

1 모음이 변하는 경우

단수	복수	단수	복수
man	men	woman	women
foot	feet	tooth	teeth
goose	geese	mouse	mice

2 어미에 -en이 붙는 경우

단수	복수	단수	복수
ox	oxen	child	children

3 단수형과 복수형이 같은 경우

단수	복수	단수	복수
fish	fish	sheep	sheep
deer	deer	Chinese	Chinese

TIP

명사의 복수형 어미 –s나 –es의 발음

❶ 무성음 p, f, t, k, θ 뒤에서는 [s]로 발음한다.

stops [stɔps] (정지)　　　　　roofs [ruːfs] (지붕)

months [mʌnθs] (달)　　　　cats [kæts] (고양이)

books [buks] (책)　　　　　laughs [læfs] (웃음)

❷ 유성음 뒤에서는 [z]로 발음한다.

pens [penz] (펜)　　　　　boys [bɔiz] (소년)

beds [bedz] (침대)　　　　girls [gəːrlz] (소녀)

❸ 마찰음 s, z, ʃ, ʒ, tʃ, dʒ 뒤에서는 [iz]로 발음한다.

buses [bʌsiz] (버스)　　　　dishes [diʃiz] (접시)

churches [tʃəːrtʃiz] (교회)　　boxes [bɔksiz] (상자)

명사의 성

명사의 성은 남성, 여성, 중성, 통성 4가지가 있다.

· 남성: man, boy, father, brother 등
· 여성: woman, girl, mother, sister 등
· 중성: book, desk, pen, pencil 등 (성의 구별이 없는 말)
· 통성: student, child, baby 등 (남성, 여성에 공통으로 쓰이는 말)

Part 2 명사 Noun

1 남성명사와 여성명사

1 남성명사에 -ess를 붙여 여성명사를 만드는 경우

· prince – prin**cess**   · lion – lion**ess**   · waiter – wait**ress**

2 성을 나타내는 말이 앞에 붙는 경우

· boyfriend – girlfriend   · manservant – maidservant

3 전혀 다른 말을 사용할 경우

· father – mother   · brother – sister   · man – woman

2 주의할 명사의 성   명사를 대명사로 받을 때 남성은 he, 여성은 she, 중성은 it, 통성은 it(he, she)으로 받는다.

1 **남성으로 취급하는 명사**   강하고 웅대하고 무서운 것

sun, war, winter, ocean, death 등

· The **sun** has **his** heat and light **himself**.

2 **여성으로 취급하는 명사**   아름답고 평화롭고 순한 것

the moon, the earth, nature, hope 등

· The **moon** has **her** beautiful shape.

3 선박은 여성명사 취급을 한다.

· The **ship** sank with **her** crew and passengers.

4 국명, 도시 이름은 여성명사 취급을 한다. 국토의 이름은 중성 취급을 한다.

· **England** is proud of **her** poets.
· **Korea** is famous for **its** blue sky.

5 통성명사 baby, child는 it으로 받기도 하나 성을 알 때에는 he, she로 받는다.

· The **baby** has a doll in **its** hand.
· The **child** plays with **his** friend.
· A true **friend** can have **his** true friend.

▶▶ friend의 성을 알 때에는 he, she로 받는다.

명사의 격

1. **Chanho** is a good student. (주격)	찬호는 훌륭한 학생이다.
2. I like **Chanho**. (목적격)	나는 찬호를 좋아한다.
3. **Chanho**'s friend is good. (소유격)	찬호의 친구는 착하다.

명사가 다른 어구에 대하여 갖는 관계를 격이라고 한다. 격에는 주격, 목적격, 소유격 3가지가 있다.

1 주격의 용법 문장의 주어, 주격보어, 호격으로 쓰인다.

· **The doctor** is very kind.   (주어)
· He is **a doctor**. (he = a doctor)   (주격보어)
· Come here, **Tom**.   (호격)

2 목적격의 용법 동사의 목적어, 전치사의 목적어, 동족목적어, 목적격보어로 쓰인다.

· I like **Seoul**.   (동사의 목적어)
· I live **in Seoul**.   (전치사의 목적어)
· I live a happy **life**.   (동족목적어)
· We call the city **Seoul**.   (목적격보어)

3 소유격의 용법 소유의 뜻을 나타내는 말로 명사 뒤에 's를 붙인다.

· This is **Jane**'s friend.
· This is my **father**'s friend.

TIP 명사의 소유격은 사람과 동물의 소유격에만 's를 붙인다. 명사의 주격과 목적격은 형태가 같다.
· **The dog** is mine.   (주어)
· I like **the dog**.   (목적어)
· **The dog's** house is beautiful.   (소유격)

4 소유격을 만드는 방법

1 사람과 동물의 소유격은 명사 뒤에 's를 붙인다. 그리고 복수명사 뒤에는 '(아포스트로피)만을 붙인다.

- the **girl's** friend (그 소녀의 친구)
- the **girls'** school (그 여학교)
- the **child's** doll (그 아이의 인형)
- the **children's** dolls (그 아이들의 인형들)
- the **boy's** book (그 소년의 책)
- the **boys'** books (그 소년들의 책들)
- **Tom's** friend (톰의 친구)
- **Tom's** friends (톰의 친구들)

2 무생물의 소유격은 〈of + 명사〉로 표현한다. 식물도 무생물 소유격 방법으로 표현한다.

- the table's legs (×) ➡ the legs **of** the table (○)
- the tree's leaves (×) ➡ the leaves **of** the tree (○)

▶▶ 무생물에도 시간, 거리, 무게, 의인화 등의 경우는 's를 붙인다.

- **today's** paper   (시간)
- five **tons'** weight   (무게)
- five **miles'** distance   (거리)
- the **world's** history   (의인화)

3 **이중소유격**   소유격이 a(an), this, that, some, any 등과 함께 나란히 쓰일 수 없기 때문에 〈of + 독립소유격〉을 명사 뒤에 둔다.

- a my father's friend   (×)
  my father's a friend   (×)
  a friend of **my father's** (○)
- this my mother's book   (×)
  my mother's this book   (×)
  this book **of my mother's** (○)

4 **소유격 뒤의 명사 생략**

① 앞에 나온 명사의 반복을 피하기 위하여 소유격 뒤에서 명사를 생략한다.
- This book is my **sister's** (book).

② 소유격의 다음에 house, shop, store, office 등이 소유격의 명사 뒤에 올 때 이를 생략한다.
- I go to my **uncle's** (house).
- He went to the **bookseller's** (store).
- I went to the **barber's** (shop).

Pattern Practice

1. This is **a** little **dog**.

2. These are little **dogs**.

3. **The cat** is clever.

4. **The cats** are clever.

5. There is **an elephant** in the zoo.

6. There are **elephants** in the zoo.

7. My father has **a sheep**.

8. My father has many **sheep**.

9. My **trousers** are very large.

10. I bought **a pair of trousers** yesterday.

11. She is ten **years** old.

12. She is a ten-**year**-old girl.

13. I met a **poet** and a **poetess**.

14. I like the **man**. / **He** is kind.

15. I like the **lady**. / **She** is kind.

16. I like the **book**. / **It** is interesting.

17. I like the **teacher**. / **He(She)** is kind and good.

18. I like the **baby**. / **It(He, She)** is very pretty.

19. The **nature** has **her** beauty.

20. I met an old friend **of my father's**.

연습문제

1. 다음 영문을 우리말로 옮기시오.

(1) My brother watches the sheep. _____

(2) I bought a pair of glasses. _____

(3) I met a poet and a teacher. _____

(4) I met a poet and teacher. _____

(5) He goes to his uncle's. _____

(6) The sun has his heat and light himself. _____

(7) Korea is famous for its scenery. _____

(8) He is a ten-year-old boy. _____

(9) The ship sank with her crew and passengers. _____

(10) I met an old friend of my father's. _____

(11) The cat is very clever. _____

(12) The cats are very clever. _____

(13) There is an apple in the basket. _____

(14) There are some apples in the basket. _____

(15) I met my friend. _____

2. 다음 문장을 영작하시오.

(1) 나는 어머니의 옛 친구 한 분을 만났다. _____

(2) 그는 12살이다. _____

(3) 책상 위에 책 한 권이 있다. _____

(4) 나는 나의 아저씨 집에 갔다. _____

(5) 그녀는 그녀의 친구를 만났다. _____

3. 다음 명사의 복수형을 쓰시오.

(1) book　　　　　_____

(2) baby　　　　　_____

(3) boy　　　　　　_____

(4) girl　　　　　　_____

(5) bench　　　　　_____

(6) knife　　　　　_____

(7) roof　　　　　_____

(8) goose　　　　_____

(9) man　　　　　_____

(10) boyfriend　　_____

4. 다음 복수형의 어미 –(e)s의 발음을 [s], [z], [iz]로 구별하시오.

(1) books　　　　[　　　　　　　　　]

(2) houses　　　　[　　　　　　　　　]

(3) dogs　　　　　[　　　　　　　　　]

(4) ladies　　　　[　　　　　　　　　]

(5) cats　　　　　[　　　　　　　　　]

(6) benches　　　[　　　　　　　　　]

(7) boys　　　　　[　　　　　　　　　]

(8) leaves　　　　[　　　　　　　　　]

(9) babies　　　　[　　　　　　　　　]

(10) potatoes　　[　　　　　　　　　]

(11) roofs　　　　[　　　　　　　　　]

(12) stops　　　　[　　　　　　　　　]

(13) boxes　　　　[　　　　　　　　　]

(14) girls　　　　　[　　　　　　　　　]

(15) buses　　　　[　　　　　　　　　]

연습문제

5. 다음 문장에서 잘못된 곳을 바르게 고치시오.

(1) I met my a father's friend.

_____

(2) He went to his uncle.

_____

(3) The boys's teacher is kind.

_____

(4) This my father's book is very interesting.

_____

(5) My house's roof is green.

_____

6. 다음 각 단어의 반대되는 단어를 쓰시오.

(1) father _____

(2) sister _____

(3) aunt _____

(4) man _____

(5) prince _____

(6) boyfriend _____

(7) manservant _____

(8) lion _____

(9) nephew _____

(10) ox _____

1. 다음 문장을 복수형으로 고친 것 중 잘못된 곳을 바르게 고치시오.

(1) He has a knife in his hand. ➡ They have a knives in their hands.

_____

(2) There is a baby in the room. ➡ There are babys in the rooms.

_____

(3) You are a good friend. ➡ You are good friend.

_____

(4) The boy has milk for breakfast. ➡ The boys have milks for breakfast.

_____

2. 다음 문장에서 잘못된 곳을 바르게 고치시오.

(1) These are the boys's book.　　_____

(2) The car's color is red.　　_____

(3) This is my father's a car.　　_____

(4) Tom and Mary's books are not easy.　_____

(5) I saw a five-years-old girl.　　_____

(6) There is a lot of benches in the park.　_____

3. 다음 한글의 뜻을 영어로 쓰시오.

(1) 나의 친구　　_____

(2) 나의 아버지의 친구　　_____

(3) 나의 아버지의 한 친구　　_____

(4) 톰의 친구　　_____

(5) 그 책상의 다리들　　_____

(6) 오늘의 신문　　_____

Part 3

관사

ARTICLE

부정관사의 용법

P·r·e·v·i·e·w

1. He is **a** student.	그는 학생이다.
2. There are four seasons in **a** year.	일 년에 사계절이 있다.
3. **An** old man came to see you.	어떤 노인이 당신을 만나러 왔다.
4. We are all of **an** age.	우리는 모두 같은 나이다.
5. I write a letter to my parents once **a** month.	나는 부모님께 한 달에 한 번 편지를 쓴다.
6. **A** dog is a faithful animal.	개는 충실한 동물이다.

관사에는 부정관사(a, an)와 정관사(the)가 있다. 관사는 항상 명사 앞에 쓰이는 일종의 형용사이다. a, an은 가산명사 앞에 단수인 경우에만 사용한다. 막연하게 '하나'라는 의미를 갖고 있다. a는 자음 발음 앞에, an은 모음발음 앞에 온다. 철자와는 관계가 없다.

a book	**an** apple	**a** boy – **an** honest boy
a pen	**an** album	**an** animal – **a** useful animal
a European	**an** M.P.	**a** man – **an** old man

1 **막연한 '하나'** 이때 보통 우리말로 해석하지 않는다.

- This is **a** book.
- That is **an** old book.

2 **특정한 '하나(one)'** 이때에는 '하나'의 뜻으로 해석한다.

- There are seven days in **a** week.
- Rome was not built in **a** day.

3 **'어떤(a certain)'**

- I met **a** Mr. Kim on the street.
- Once there lived **an** old man in a town.

4 **'같은(the same)'**

- They are all of **a** size.
- Birds of **a** feather flock together.
  - ▶▶ ⟨of + a(an) + 명사⟩의 경우, a(an)는 '같은(the same)'의 뜻으로 쓰인다.

5 '~마다(per)'

- I write to him about once **a** month.
- How many cups of coffee do you have **a** day?

  ▶▶ 이때에는 a(an)가 전치사의 역할을 겸하기 때문에 전치사 in(at, on)이 필요 없다.

6 '~라는 것(어떤 ~라도)' 종족 전체를 대표하는 경우에 쓰인다.

- **A dog** is a faithful animal.
- **Dogs** are faithful animals.

TIP

부정관사와 정관사의 비교

- There is a book on the desk. (책상 위에 책이 있다.)
- The book on the desk is mine. (책상 위에 있는 그 책은 나의 것이다.)

- Give me a red pencil. (빨간색의 연필 중에서 하나를 말한다.)
- Give me the red pencil. (여러 가지 색의 연필 중에서 빨간 색의 연필)

부정관사는 일반적으로 불특정한 하나를 나타내는 말로 가산명사 앞에 쓰이고, 정관사는 특정한 명사 앞에 쓰인다.

부정관사를 포함한 관용어

a great many (다수의)	**a** great deal of (다량의)
in **a** hurry (서둘러)	as **a** rule (대개, 일반적으로)
have **a** cold (감기에 걸리다)	as **a** whole (전체적으로)

정관사의 용법

1. I saw a boy. **The** boy was handsome.	나는 소년을 보았다. 그 소년은 잘생겼다.
2. Please open **the** door.	문 좀 열어 주세요.
3. **The** pen on the table is mine.	탁자 위에 있는 펜은 나의 것이다.
4. **The** sun is larger than the moon.	태양은 달보다 크다.
5. Sunday is **the** first day of the week.	일요일은 일주일의 첫째 날이다.
6. **The** dog is a faithful animal.	개는 충실한 동물이다.
7. He took me by **the** hand.	그는 나의 손을 잡았다.
8. **The** rich are not always happy.	부자들이 반드시 행복한 것은 아니다.
9. I get up early in **the** morning.	나는 아침에 일찍 일어난다.

정관사 the는 '그'라는 가벼운 뜻으로 해석하고 특정한 것을 가리킬 때 가산명사나 불가산명사 앞에 붙여 모두 쓰인다. 또 단수명사와 복수명사 앞에도 모두 쓰인다.

- **The** boy plays baseball.　　　(가산명사 단수)
- **The** boys play baseball.　　　(가산명사 복수)
- She gave me **the** book.　　　(가산명사 단수)
- She gave me **the** money.　　　(불가산명사)

TIP　정관사 the는 자음 앞에서는 [ðə], 모음 앞에서는 [ði]로 발음한다.
- I like **the** book.
- I like **the** apple.

1 앞에 나온 명사가 다시 나올 때

- There is a book on the desk. **The** book is mine.
- I saw a girl. **The** girl is Tom's sister.

2 서로 알고 있는 것을 가리킬 때

- Will you open **the** window?
- Please look at **the** blackboard.

3 수식어구에 의해 한정될 때

· **The** book on the desk is his.
· **The** book which I read is hers.

4 서수나 최상급의 형용사 앞에

· Monday is **the** second day of the week.
· Junho is **the** tallest boy in his class.

5 세상에서 유일한 것을 가리킬 때

· **The** sun is larger than **the** moon.
· **The** sky is clear in autumn.

6 종족 전체를 나타낼 때

· **The** dog is a faithful animal.
· **A** dog is a faithful animal.
· **Dogs** are faithful animals.

7 계량의 단위를 나타낼 때

· Sugar is sold by **the** pound.
· They sell cloths by **the** yard.

8 대명사의 소유격 대용에

· He took me by **the** hand.
· He hit me on **the** head.

9 the + 형용사 = 복수명사를 만들 때

· **The** rich are not always happy.

10 관용어구에

· in **the** morning, in **the** park, on **the** street 등

1. I am **a** student.

2. **The** student is Korean.

3. I met **a** handsome boy at school.

4. Please give me **a** glass of water.

5. **A** lady has been waiting for you for two hours.

6. These boys are **of an** age.

7. How many cups of coffee do you have **a** day?

8. **A** cat is a clever animal.

9. I met a lady. **The** lady is beautiful.

10. Please close **the** door.

11. **The** watch made in Korea is good.

12. **The** watch which I bought yesterday is good.

13. He was **the** first Korean to come to this country.

14. He is **the** shortest boy in his class.

15. **The** moon is beautiful all the time.

16. **The** cat is a clever animal.

17. Coffee is sold by **the** pound.

18. She took me by **the** hand.

19. **The** poor are not always unhappy.

20. I have lunch in **the** afternoon.

연습문제

1. 다음 영문을 우리말로 옮기시오.

(1) I saw a boy on the playground. The boy was a good tennis player.

_____

(2) There are twelve months in a year. _____

(3) A gentleman came to meet you yesterday. _____

(4) They are all of a business. _____

(5) I have three meals a day. _____

(6) A fox is a cunning animal. _____

(7) January is the first month of the year. _____

(8) She took me by the hand. _____

(9) The rich are not always happy. _____

(10) She plays the violin very well. _____

2. 다음 ( ) 안에 a, an, the를 써 넣으시오. 필요 없는 곳에는 ×표를 하시오.

(1) There is ( ) book on the desk.

(2) There is ( ) apple in the basket.

(3) There are ( ) lot of people in the park.

(4) There are ( ) lots of people in the park.

(5) Please go to ( ) blackboard.

(6) ( ) sun is larger than ( ) moon.

(7) He is ( ) tallest boy in the class.

(8) I get up early in ( ) morning.

(9) ( ) watch made in Korea is very good.

(10) He plays ( ) baseball.

(11) She plays ( ) piano.

(12) She has milk for ( ) breakfast.

(13) ( ) coffee is sold by ( ) pound.

03 정관사와 고유명사

고유명사 앞에는 관사를 붙이지 않으나, 다음과 같은 경우에는 the를 붙인다.

1 관공서, 공공건물 앞에

- **the** White House (백악관), **the** National Museum (국립박물관)

  ▶▶ 역명, 호수명, 공원명에는 일반적으로 the를 붙이지 않는다.
  - Seoul Station, Lake Soyang, Pagoda Park 등

2 강, 바다 이름 앞에

- **the** Han River, **the** Pacific 등

3 산맥, 반도 이름 앞에

- **the** Rocky Mountains, **the** Korean Peninsula 등

4 신문, 잡지 이름 앞에

- **the** New York Times, **the** Newsweek 등

5 배, 기차 이름 앞에

- **the** Car Ferry, **the** KTX 등

6 나라 이름 앞에 (연합국가)

- **the** United States of America 등

04 관사의 생략과 반복

명사와 명사가 and로 이어질 때 and 뒤에 관사가 있을 때와 생략할 경우 뜻이 다르다.

- **A** teacher and **a** poet are present at the meeting. (다른 인물)
  선생님과 시인이 그 회의에 참석하고 있다.

- **A** teacher and poet is present at the meeting. (동일 인물)
  선생님이고 시인인 분이 회의에 참석하고 있다.

Chapter 05 관사의 위치

1. He is **a** very honest boy.	그는 매우 정직한 소년이다.
2. All **the** boys are very honest.	소년들 모두가 매우 정직하다.
3. **How** pretty a doll this is!	이것은 참 예쁜 인형이구나!
4. She must be foolish to marry **such a** man.	그녀가 그런 남자와 결혼하다니 바보임에 틀림없다.

1 〈관사 + (부사 + 형용사) + 명사〉 일반적인 어순이다.

· This is **a** very interesting book.

2 〈all(both) + the + 명사〉

· I spent **all the** money.
· I like **all the** boys.
· **Both the** parents are still alive.

3 〈how(too, so, as) + 형용사 + a + 명사〉

· **How** beautiful **a** flower this is!
· I bought **too** small **a** house.
· I never saw **so** tall **a** man.
· Tom is **as** wise **a** boy as Mary.

4 〈such(quite, what) + a + 형용사 + 명사〉

· You cannot finish the work **such a** short time.
· We went on a picnic on **quite a** fine day.
· **What a** beautiful flower this is!

관사의 생략

P · r · e · v · i · e · w

1. **Mother**, give me some milk.	어머니, 우유 좀 주세요.
2. **King** Sejong accomplished great results.	세종대왕은 훌륭한 업적들을 달성했다
3. I go to school **by bus**.	나는 학교에 버스로 간다.

다음과 같은 경우에 정관사 the를 생략한다.

1 상대방을 부를 때(호격)

· **Waiter**, give me a cup of coffee.

2 자기 가족을 가리킬 때

· I met **Father** at the office.

3 관직, 직위를 나타내는 명사가 칭호, 동격, 보어로 쓰일 때

· **President** Lincoln was one of the greatest men in the world.
· Mr. Brown, **chairman** of the company is gentle.
· We elect him **president**.

4 건물이 본래의 목적으로 쓰일 때

· I go to **school**.
· I go to **church**.

5 운동, 식사 이름 앞에

· He plays **baseball** after school.
· She has **lunch** at twelve-thirty.

6 교통수단을 나타낼 때

· I went to school **by car**.
· She went to Japan **by ship**.

7 대구를 이룰 때

· They went away **arm in arm**.

Pattern Practice

1. How far is it from **Seoul Station** to **the** National Museum?

2. **The** Korean Peninsula is located in the Far East.

3. **The** Times is a weekly magazine in America.

4. **The** United States of America has many kinds of people.

5. My teacher is **a** teacher and poet.

6. **How** nice a house this is!

7. **What a** nice house this is!

8. This is a **very** nice house.

9. **All** the boys went on a picnic last Sunday.

10. I went to the beach **by train**.

11. I go to **bed** late everyday.

12. She plays **tennis** after school.

13. She plays **the piano** in the evening.

14. We go to school **hand in hand**.

15. I had gimbap for **lunch**.

16. They elected him **president**.

17. **The president** must work for the people.

18. **Mom**, give me something to eat.

19. I went to **Mother** in Seoul.

20. She goes to **church** on Sunday.

1. 다음 ( ) 안에서 알맞은 관사를 고르시오.

(1) Here is a book. (The, A) book is mine.

(2) Seoul is (a, the) capital of Korea.

(3) I met her (a, an) hour ago.

(4) The dog is (a, an) useful animal.

(5) He has (a, an) album.

(6) (Han River, The Han River) is in Seoul.

(7) He was (a, the) first Korean who went to Hawaii.

(8) He took me by (a, the) hand.

2. 다음 영문을 우리말로 옮기시오.

(1) I met a teacher and poet. _____

(2) I met a teacher and a poet. _____

(3) Sugar is sold by the pound. _____

(4) He hit me on the head. _____

(5) The old cannot go to the mountain by themselves. _____

(6) Both the parents are still alive. _____

(7) She goes to school by bus. _____

(8) He goes to the school by car. _____

3. 다음 문장에서 잘못된 곳을 바르게 고치시오.

(1) He went to mother with his sister. _____

(2) We elected him a president. _____

(3) How a pretty girl she is! _____

(4) I never saw so a tall boy. _____

TIP

12개월

January	1월	February	2월
March	3월	April	4월
May	5월	June	6월
July	7월	August	8월
September	9월	October	10월
November	11월	December	12월

요일

Sunday	일요일	Monday	월요일
Tuesday	화요일	Wednesday	수요일
Thursday	목요일	Friday	금요일
Saturday	토요일		

계절

spring	봄	summer	여름
autumn	가을(=fall)	winter	겨울

Part 4

대명사

PRONOUN

1. I met **him** and **his** friend.	나는 그와 그의 친구를 만났다.
2. **This** is a book.	이것은 책이다.
3. I have **some** money.	나는 약간의 돈을 가지고 있다.
4. I don't know **who** she is.	나는 그녀가 누구인지 모른다.
5. I don't know the man **who** is reading a book.	나는 책을 읽고 있는 그 남자를 모른다.

명사 대신에 쓰이는 말을 대명사라고 한다. 대명사에는 인칭대명사, 지시대명사, 부정대명사, 의문대명사, 관계대명사 등 5가지 종류가 있다.

1 인칭대명사 사람을 가리키는 말이다.

· I, you, he, she, my, him 등

2 지시대명사 사람이나 사물을 가리키는 말이다.

· this(these), that(those) 등

3 부정대명사 불특정의 사람, 사물, 수량 등을 나타내는 말이다.

· one, some, any, other, each 등

4 의문대명사 의문을 나타내는 말이다.

· who, what, which

5 관계대명사 대명사와 접속사의 역할을 하는 말이다.

· who, which, that, what

인칭대명사

1 인칭대명사의 격변화

인칭	수 \ 격		주격 -은, -이	소유격 -의	목적격 -을	소유대명사 -의 것	재귀대명사 -자신
1인칭	단 수		I	my	me	mine	myself
	복 수		we	our	us	ours	ourselves
2인칭	단 수		you	your	you	yours	yourself
	복 수		you	your	you	yours	yourselves
3인칭	단수	남성	he	his	him	his	himself
		여성	she	her	her	hers	herself
		중성	it	its	it	×	itself
	복 수		they	their	them	theirs	themselves

1 인칭대명사의 구별

① 1인칭: 말하는 사람, 즉 I(we)뿐이다.

② 2인칭: 말을 듣는 사람, 즉 you(you)뿐이다.

③ 3인칭: 1인칭과 2인칭을 뺀 세상의 모든 것으로 he, she, this, that, it 등이 있다.
   주의할 것은 비록 자기의 이름이라도 3인칭에 속한다.

· **I** like **you**.   (I는 1인칭 주격, you는 2인칭 목적격)

· **You** like **me**.   (you는 2인칭 주격, me는 1인칭 목적격)

· **He** likes **her**.   (he는 3인칭 주격, her는 3인칭 목적격)

2 〈대명사 + and + 대명사〉의 용법

· **You and I** are students.	We are students.
· **He and I** are students.	We are students.
· **You, she and I** are students.	We are students.
· **They and I** are students.	We are students.
· **You and he** are students.	You are students.
· **You and they** are students.	You are students.
· **He and she** are students.	They are students.
· **He and they** are students.	They are students.

Part 4 대명사 Pronoun

2 we, you, they의 특별 용법 we, you, they 등이 막연한 일반 사람을 나타내는 경우 해석하지 않는다.

- **We** have much rain in summer.
- **You** should respect your neighbors.
- **They** speak English in Canada.
- **They** say that he is honest.

3 소유대명사의 용법 〈소유격 + 명사〉의 뜻으로 소유대명사 또는 독립소유격이라고 한다.

- This is **my** book. ➡ This book is **mine**.
- That is **his** book. ➡ That book is **his**.

소유대명사의 단수와 복수의 형태는 같다.

- This book is **mine**.
- These books are **mine**.

- This book is **ours**.
- These books are **ours**.

4 재귀대명사의 용법

1 재귀적 용법 주어진 동작이 자신에게 돌아오는 경우이며 주로 동사와 전치사의 목적어로 쓰인다. 문장에서 재귀대명사를 빼면 문장이 성립되지 않는다.

- He killed **himself**.
- He looked at **himself** in the water.

2 강조적 용법 주어나 목적어의 뜻을 강조한다. 문장에서 재귀대명사를 빼도 문장이 성립된다.

- Tom **himself** did his homework.
- I want to see Tom **himself**.

3 재귀대명사의 관용적 용법.

- He did his homework **for himself**.
- She went there **by herself**.
- The door closed **of itself**.

5 it의 특별 용법

1. There is a book. **It** is interesting. (it = the book)	책이 있다. 그것은 재미있다.
2. **It** is fine today.	오늘은 날씨가 좋다.
3. **It** is not easy **to study** English.	영어를 공부하는 것은 쉽지 않다.
4. **It** was Mary **that** I met at school.	내가 학교에서 만난 사람은 메리였다.

1 날씨, 시간, 요일, 계절, 거리, 명암 등을 나타낸다. (비인칭 대명사)

· **It** is hot today.
· What time is **it** now? **It** is seven-thirty.
· What day is **it** today? **It** is Monday today.
· What's the date? **It** is September 16.
· **It** is spring now.
· How far is it from here to your home? **It** is about a mile.
· **It** is dark now.

2 it이 가주어, 가목적어로 쓰인다.

· **It** is difficult **to learn** English. (it은 가주어, to learn 이하는 진주어)
  ➡ To learn English is difficult.

· **It** is difficult **that** we learn English. (it은 가주어, that 이하는 진주어)

· I think **it** difficult **to learn** English. (it은 가목적어, to learn 이하는 진목적어)

▶▶ 5형식에서 to부정사를 목적어로 쓸 수 없기 때문에 그 자리에 it(가목적어)을 쓰고 to부정사(진목적어)를 뒤에 놓는다.

3 **It is ~ that**의 강조 구문 〈It is + 강조하는 말 + that〉의 형식을 쓴다.

· I met Mary at school yesterday.
  ➡ It was **I** that met Mary at school yesterday. (주어 I를 강조)
  ➡ It was **Mary** that I met at school yesterday. (목적어 Mary를 강조)
  ➡ It was **at school** that I met Mary yesterday. (at school을 강조)
  ➡ It was **yesterday** that I met Mary at school. (yesterday를 강조)

Pattern Practice

1. **He** painted **himself** in a school uniform.

2. **My** sister **herself** made a pretty doll.

3. **We** have a lot of snow in winter.

4. **They** say that the earth is round.

5. **Her** brother studied English for **himself**.

6. **I** met an old friend of **my** father's.

7. **I** want to have this book of **his**.

8. **I** bought a car and gave **it** to **my** son.

9. **It** is cloudy today. I want to stay at home.

10. What time is **it** now? **It** is seven o'clock.

11. How long does **it** take to go to your home?

12. **It** takes about thirty minutes.

13. **It** is difficult for him to learn English.

14. **It** is kind of him to say so.

15. **It** is certain that he will leave soon.

16. I believe **it** good to get up early.

17. I believe **it** good that you study hard.

18. **It was** Mary **who** I saw at the supermarket.

19. **It was** at the supermarket **that** I saw Mary.

20. **It** is fine this morning, isn't it?

연습문제

1. 다음 ( ) 안에서 알맞은 것을 고르시오.

(1) I played tennis with (her, hers).

(2) I met an old friend of (her, hers).

(3) He is taller than (she, her).

(4) She likes (I, me) better than (he, him).

(5) This book is not his, but (my, mine).

2. 다음 영문에서 it의 용법을 쓰고 우리말로 옮기시오.

(1) How far is it from here to your home?   (   )

_____

(2) It is cold in winter.   (   )

_____

(3) It is difficult to learn English.   (   )

_____

(4) I think it easy to study English.   (   )

_____

(5) It was yesterday that I met her at the park.   (   )

_____

3. 밑줄 친 부분을 하나의 대명사로 고치시오.

(1) He and I are good friends.   _____

(2) You and she went to school by bus.   _____

(3) He and she are playing tennis after school.   _____

(4) He, she and I are good students.   _____

(5) This and that are good books.   _____

4. 다음 (   ) 안에 알맞은 말을 써 넣으시오.

(1) (   ) have much snow in winter.

(2) What (   ) is it today? It is Sunday today.

(3) What is the (   ) today? It is the 27th of January.

(4) (   ) is getting dark.

(5) He did his homework for (   ).

5. 다음을 영어로 옮기시오.

(1) 여름에 비가 많이 온다.　　　　_____

(2) 사람은 이웃을 존중해야한다.　_____

(3) 톰은 스스로 숙제를 했다.　　　_____

(4) 이 책은 그의 것이다.　　　　　_____

(5) 이것은 그의 학교이다.　　　　　_____

지시대명사

P · r · e · v · i · e · w

1. **This** is longer than **that**.	이것은 저것보다 더 길다.
2. I am going to read **this** book **this** week.	나는 이번 주에 이 책을 읽을 예정이다.
3. The climate of Korea is colder than **that** of Japan.	한국의 기후는 일본의 기후보다 더 춥다.
4. Work and play are both necessary to health; **this** gives us rest, and **that** gives us energy.	일과 놀이는 둘 다 건강에 필요하다. 후자(놀이)는 우리에게 휴식을 주고, 전자(일)는 활력을 준다.
5. Heaven helps **those** who help themselves.	하늘은 스스로 돕는 자를 돕는다.

---

1 this와 that의 용법

1 this는 가까운 것을 가리키고, that은 먼 것을 가리킨다. 또 지시대명사 this와 that은 사물과 사람을 가리킨다.

· **This** is my book, and **that** is his book.
· **This** is my father, and **that** is her father.

2 this와 that이 명사 앞에서 지시형용사로 쓰이고, 때를 나타내는 명사 앞에서 this는 현재의 뜻으로 that은 과거의 뜻으로 쓰인다.

· **This** book is mine, and **that** book is his.
· I will go to the beach **this** year.
· I met her in Seoul **that** year.

> **TIP**
>
> | | | | |
> |---|---|---|---|
> | **this** morning | (오늘 아침) | **that** morning | (그날 아침) |
> | in **these** days | (요즈음) | in **those** days | (그 당시) |
> | **this** week | (이번 주) | **this** winter | (올 겨울) |

3 명사의 반복을 피하기 위해 that, those가 쓰인다.

· **The winter** of Seoul is milder than **that** of Moscow.
· **The ears** of a dog are longer than **those** of a cat.

4 this(후자 = the latter)와 that(전자 = the former)의 용법

· There are a dog and a fox; **this** is cunning and **that** is faithful.

TIP this는 앞 문장에서 자신에 가까이 있는 것을 가리키고, that은 먼 곳에 있는 것을 가리킨다. 즉 this는 a fox를, that은 a dog을 가리킨다. 주의할 점은 this가 앞에 있지만 후자로, that은 뒤에 있지만 전자로 해석한다.

5 those who~   ~하는 사람들(= those people)

· **Those who** work hard will succeed.

▶▶ those는 대명사이지만 사람(people)의 뜻으로 선행사가 된다.

6 that이 앞의 문장 전체를 받는다.

· Let's go shopping now. **That**'s a good idea.

1. **This** is my book and **that** book is hers.

2. I am going to take a walk **this** morning.

3. I met her in the park **that** morning.

4. The winter of Korea is warmer than **that** of Canada.

5. How are you in **these** days?

6. They had not cars in **those** days.

7. I have a radio and a television; **this** is expensive and **that** is cheap.

8. **Those** who help others will be helped by others.

9. **That** is his car.

10. **That** car is his.

1. 다음 영문을 우리말로 옮기시오.

(1) This is my book.

_____

(2) This book is mine.

_____

(3) The winter of Seoul is colder than that of Japan.

_____

(4) I will go to school by car this morning.

_____

(5) I met him at school that morning.

_____

(6) There are a lot of people in the city in these days.

_____

(7) Those who are not diligent can not succeed.

_____

(8) The ears of a rabbit are longer than those of a dog.

_____

(9) There were not televisions in those days.

_____

(10) There are a dog and a fox; this is cunning and that is faithful.

_____

2. 다음 문장을 영작하시오.
(1) 저 자동차는 좋지 않다.   _____
(2) 저것은 좋은 자동차가 아니다.   _____
(3) 나는 내일 아침에 일찍 일어날 예정이다. _____
(4) 요즈음 어떻게 지냅니까?   _____
(5) 나는 이번 주 영어를 공부할 작정이다. _____

03 부정대명사

· P · r · e · v · i · e · w ·

1. **One** should respect **one's** parents.	사람은 부모님을 존중해야 한다.
2. Do you have a book?	당신은 책을 한 권 가지고 있습니까?
Yes, I have **one**.	예, 가지고 있습니다.
3. I have two dogs;	나는 두 마리의 개가 있습니다.
one is white and **the other** is black.	하나는 희고 다른 하나는 검습니다.
4. Do you have **any** books?	당신은 책을 좀 가지고 있습니까?
Yes, I have **some** books.	예, 책을 좀 가지고 있습니다.
5. **Each** has his own book.	각자는 자기 자신의 책을 가지고 있다.
6. **Both** of his parents are happy.	그의 부모 두 분 다 행복하다.
7. **All** of us are not happy.	우리 모두가 행복한 것은 아니다.

Part 4 대명사 Pronoun

1 one의 용법   one의 소유격은 one's이고, 목적격은 one이고, 복수는 ones이고, 재귀대명사는 oneself 이다.

1 일반 사람을 나타낼 때 쓰인다.

- **One** should keep **one's** promise.
- **One** must like **oneself**.

2 앞에 나온 명사의 반복을 피하기 위해 쓰인다.

- I have three apples; a red **one** and two yellow **ones**.
- Do you need a book? Yes, I need **one**.
- Do you need the book? Yes, I need **it**.

2 other, others, another의 용법

1 one, the other (둘 중의)   하나는 ~이고, 나머지 하나는 ~이다.

- Here are two dogs; **one** is mine and **the other** is hers.

2 one, another, the third (셋 중에서)   하나는 ~이고, 또 하나는 ~이고, 나머지 하나는 ~이다.

- I have three balls. **One** is red and **another** is white, and **the third** is black.

3 one, the others (셋 이상에서는)   하나는 ~이고, 그 나머지는 모두 ~이다.

- Here are many dogs. **One** is my friend's and **the others** are mine.

4 some, others (많은 것을 막연히 두 개로 나눌 때) ~도 있고, ~도 있다.

- There are a lot of flowers. **Some** are white and **others** are red.
  ▶ the others는 지정된 나머지를, others는 막연한 나머지를 가리킨다.

5 another 다른 하나, 하나 더

- I don't like this blouse. Show me **another**.
- May I have **another** egg?

6 each other (둘의 경우) 서로서로, one another (셋 이상의 경우) 서로서로

- He and she love **each other**.
- All the girls love **one another**.

3 some, any의 용법

1 some은 긍정문에, any는 의문문, 부정문, 조건문에 쓰인다.

- I have **some** books. I have **some** money.   (긍정문)
- Do you have **any** books?   (의문문)
- I don't have **any** books.   (부정문)
- If you have **any** money, lend me **some**.   (조건문)
  ▶ some과 any는 '좀, 몇 개'의 뜻으로 수와 양 모두에 쓰인다.

2 권유와 부탁할 때, 긍정의 대답을 예상할 때에는 의문문에도 some을 쓴다.

- Would you like **some** coffee?
- Will you give me **some** water?

3 〈some + 보통 단수명사〉의 경우 some이 '어떤'의 뜻으로 쓰인다.

- I read about it in **some** book.   (some + 단수명사)
- I want to read **some** books.   (some + 복수명사)

4 any가 긍정문 앞에 쓰이면 '어떤 ~라도'의 뜻으로 쓰인다.

- **Any** girl can play after school.

4 all, each, every의 용법

1 all 모든 사람의 뜻일 경우 복수로 쓰이고, 모든 것의 뜻일 경우는 단수로 쓰인다.

- **All** are busy. (모두들 바쁘다.)   (복수)
- **All** is over. (모든 것이 끝났다.)   (단수)
- **All** of them are kind. (그들 모두가 친절하다.)   (복수)

2 each(각각의), every(개개의 중점을 둔 모든) 둘 다 단수로 쓰인다.

- **Each** has his own book. (각자는 자기 자신의 책을 가지고 있다.)
- **Every** child has his own room. (모든 아이는 자기 자신의 방을 가지고 있다.)

5 both, either, neither의 용법

1 both(둘 다), both A and B(A와 B 둘 다)

- **Both** of them are kind.
- **Both** Tom **and** Mary are kind.

2 either(둘 중 어느 하나), neither(어느 쪽도 ~아니다)

- **Either** of my friends is kind.
- **Neither** of my friends is kind.

▶▶ either와 neither 둘 다 단수로 쓰인다.

6 부분부정과 전체부정의 용법 일부는 긍정하고, 일부는 부정하는 경우를 부분부정이라고 한다. every, all, both, always 등이 not과 같이 쓰여 '~인 것은 아니다'로 해석한다.

- **Everybody** does **not** like music. (누구나 음악을 좋아하는 것은 아니다.) (부분부정)
  Nobody likes music. (아무도 음악을 좋아하지 않는다.)   (전체부정)

- I don't like **all** of them. (내가 그들 모두를 좋아하는 것은 아니다.) (부분부정)
  I don't like any of them. (나는 그들 중 어느 누구도 좋아하지 않는다.) (전체부정)

- **Both** of them are **not** busy. (그들 둘 다 바쁘지 않다.)   (부분부정)
  Either of them is not busy. (그들 중 어느 하나도 바쁘지 않다.)   (전체부정)

- I am **not always** busy. (나는 항상 바쁜 것은 아니다.)   (부분부정)

Pattern Practice

1. **One** always loves **one's** children.

2. I have two sons. **One** is a doctor and **the other** is a teacher.

3. I have three sons. **One** is a farmer, **another** a doctor, and **the third** a teacher.

4. There are some students in the library. **One** is listening to music and **the others** are studying hard.

5. There are many students on the playground. **Some** are playing tennis and **others** are playing baseball.

6. I don't like this cap. Would you show me **another**?

7. Would you have **another** cup of coffee?

8. Tom and Mary looked at **each other**.

9. All the students helped **one another**.

10. There are **some** books on the desk.

11. Are there **any** books on the desk?

12. There are not **any** books on the desk.

13. If you have **any** books, lend me **some**.

14. Would you give me **some** money?

15. I found it in **some** book.

16. **Any** child can solve the problem.

17. I gave him **all** the books.

18. I gave him **all** the money.

19. **Each** has his own desk.

20. **Each** boy has his own desk.

21. **Every** boy has his own desk.

22. **Both** (of them) are diligent.

23. **Both** the boys are diligent.

24. **Both** Tom **and** Mary are diligent.

25. **Either** you **or** he is wrong.

26. **Neither** you **nor** I am wrong.

27. **Both** of them are **not** wrong.

28. **Not all** men are good.

1. 다음 영문을 우리말로 옮기시오.

(1) One should keep one's promise. _____

(2) I have two brothers; one is a teacher and the other is a doctor.

_____

(3) I have many books. One is easy and the others are not easy.

_____

(4) I have many books. Some are easy and others are not easy.

_____

(5) I don't like this brush. Will you show me another?

_____

(6) Do you have any flowers in your garden? _____

(7) I have some flowers in my garden. _____

(8) I don't have any flowers in my garden. _____

(9) Would you like some coffee? _____

(10) If you have any money, lend him some. _____

(11) Tom and Mary helped each other. _____

(12) They helped one another. _____

(13) Either you or he is wrong. _____

(14) Neither you nor I am wrong. _____

(15) Both of them are not wrong. _____

2. 다음 문장을 영작하시오.

(1) 엄마, 계란 하나 더 먹어도 되요? _____

(2) 우유 좀 드시겠어요? _____

(3) 나는 돈이 한 푼도 없다. _____

(4) 그와 그녀는 서로 사랑한다. _____

(5) 부자가 반드시 행복한 것은 아니다. _____

3. 다음 ( ) 안에서 알맞은 말을 고르시오.

(1) There (are, is) some books in the room.

(2) There (are, is) some money in the pocket.

(3) All (are, is) busy.

(4) All (are, is) over.

(5) All of us (are, is) diligent.

(6) Each of the students (are, is) diligent.

(7) Every boy and every girl (are, is) diligent.

(8) Both of them (are, is) kind.

(9) Either of them (are, is) busy.

(10) Neither of them (are, is) busy.

(11) Either you or he (are, is) busy.

(12) Neither he nor you (are, is) busy.

4. 다음 ( ) 안에 알맞은 말을 써 넣으시오.

(1) One should love (   ) parents.

(2) Do you have a pen? Yes, I have (   ).

(3) Do you have the pen? Yes, I have (   ).

(4) You have two sons; one is a teacher and (   ) (   ) is a doctor.

(5) They love one (   ).

(6) We love each (   ).

(7) He did his homework (   ) himself.

(8) She sat by the window (   ) herself.

(9) I don't like this book. Please show me (   ).

(10) I have three balls; one is white and (   ) is red, and the (   ) is black.

(11) There are many students here; one is diligent and the (   ) are busy.

(12) Do you have any money? Yes, I have (   ).

(13) Do you have any books? No, I don't have (   ).

Chapter 04 의문사

P · r · e · v · i · e · w

1. **Who** is he?	그는 누구입니까?
2. **What** do you want?	당신은 무엇을 원합니까?
3. **Which** do you like better, an apple or an orange?	사과와 귤 중에서 어느 것을 더 좋아합니까?
4. **When** does he start?	그는 언제 떠납니까?
5. **Where** does she study?	그녀는 어디서 공부를 합니까?
6. **How** do you go to school?	당신은 학교에 어떻게 갑니까?
7. **Why** were you late yesterday?	당신은 어제 왜 늦었습니까?

의문사 분류

- **의문대명사**   who, whose, whom, what, which
- **의문형용사**   what, which
- **의문부사**   where, when, how, why 등

1 who, whose, whom의 용법

사람의 이름이나 혈족 관계를 물어볼 때 쓰인다. who는 주격, whose는 소유격, whom은 목적격이다. 의문대명사는 단수와 복수에 다 같이 쓰이고, 의문대명사가 주어이면 조동사 do, does, did 등이 필요 없다.

- **Who** is she? She is **Mary**.　　　(이름)
- **Who** is she? She is my **sister**.　　(가족 관계)

- **Whose** book is this? It is my book.　(소유격)
- **Whose** is this book? It is mine.　　(소유대명사)

- **Whom**(**Who**) do you like?　　(동사의 목적어)
- **With whom** do you play?　　(전치사의 목적어)
- **Whom** do you play **with**?　　(전치사의 목적어)
- **Who** do you play **with**?　　(전치사의 목적어)

▸▸ 회화체에서는 whom 대신에 who가 많이 쓰인다.

2 what, which의 용법

1 what은 사물이나 사람의 직업 또는 신분을 물을 때 쓰인다.

- **What** is she? She is a teacher.   (직업/의문대명사)
- **What** is this? It is a story book.   (사물/의문대명사)
- **What** book is this? It is a story book.   (사물/의문형용사)

2 which는 한정된 범위에서 '어느 것'의 뜻으로 사물과 사람 양쪽에 쓰인다.

- **Which** of them do you like best?
- **Which** of them can drive a car?
- **Which** book do you like best?

▶▶ what은 정해져 있지 않은 것 중에서 '무엇'으로, which는 정해진 것 중에서 '어느 것'의 뜻으로 쓰인다.

3 when, where의 용법

1 when은 '언제'의 뜻으로 때를 나타내는 부사로 쓰이나, 동사와 전치사의 목적어로 쓰이기도 한다.

- **When** is your birthday? My birthday is September 16.
- **When** and **where** were you born?

2 where은 '어디서'의 뜻으로 장소를 나타내는 부사로 쓰이나, 동사와 전치사의 목적어로 쓰이기도 한다.

- **Where** do you live? I live in Seoul.
- Please tell me **when** and **where**.

4 how, why의 용법

1 how는 '어떻게'의 뜻으로는 방법을 나타내고, 형용사나 부사와 같이 '얼마나'의 뜻으로는 정도를 나타낸다.

- **How** do you go to school? I go to school **by bus**.   (방법)
- **How** long are you staying there?   (정도)

2 why는 '왜'라고 이유를 물을 때 쓰인다. 이때 대답은 because로 한다.

- **Why** were you absent yesterday? **Because** I was sick.
- **Why** do you come here? **To** learn English.

Pattern Practice

1. **Who** is that lady?   She is **Miss Brown**.

2. **Who** is that lady?   She is **my sister**.

3. **What** is that lady?   She is **a teacher**.

4. **Whose** desk is this?   It is **her** desk.

5. **Whose** is this desk?   It is **hers**.

6. **Who** do you like?   I like **him**.

7. With **whom** do you play?   I play with **Tom**.

8. **What** do you like best?   I like **a book** best.

9. **Which** of them do you like best?   I like **the book** best.

10. **When** is her birthday?   Her birthday is **January 27**.

11. **When** does he get up?   He gets up **at six in the morning**.

12. **Where** is your house?   My house is **in Seoul**.

13. **Where** do you live?   I live **in Seoul**.

14. **How** do you go to school?   I go to school **by car**.

15. **How long** has she been waiting for?   She has been waiting **for an hour**.

16. **Why** does the girl cry?   **Because** she wants to see her mother.

17. **Why** were you late?   **Because** I got up late.

18. **Where** did he buy the car?   He bought it **in Busan**.

19. **Where** were you born?   I was born **in America**.

20. **What** color do you like?   I like **white**.

연습문제

1 다음 영문을 우리말로 옮기시오.

(1) Which do you like better, this one or that one?

_____

(2) Whose bag is this?　　_____

(3) Whose is this bag?　　_____

(4) What does he want to have?　　_____

(5) What book does she want to have?_____

(6) When did you buy that car?　　_____

(7) I don't know when he will leave Seoul._____

(8) Today is the day when I was born._____

(9) My mother was happy when my brother was born.

_____

(10) How far is it from here to your school?　_____

(11) How long does it take to go to your school?

_____

(12) Why were you absent yesterday?_____

(13) Where are you going?　_____

(14) Where are you going to read this book?　_____

(15) When are you leaving Seoul?　_____

2 다음 문장을 영작하시오.

(1) 너는 어디에 사니?　　_____

(2) 그녀는 언제 떠날 예정이니?　_____

(3) 너는 어제 왜 늦었니?　_____

(4) 그녀는 무엇을 원하니?　_____

(5) 이것이 내가 태어난 그 집이다._____

3 다음 두 문장의 뜻이 같도록 (   ) 안에 알맞은 말을 써 넣으시오.

(1) (   ) does Mr. Brown live? He lives in New York.

(2) (   ) did he want to do? He wanted to read some books.

(3) (   ) is she? She is Miss Brown.

(4) (   ) is she? She is a doctor.

(5) (   ) is she? She is my mother.

(6) (   ) broke the window? Tom broke the window.

(7) (   ) do you want to see? I want to see Mr. Brown.

(8) (   ) mother do you want to see? I want to see her mother.

(9) (   ) does she go to school? She goes to school by bus.

(10) (   ) were you absent? Because I was sick.

4 다음 두 문장을 연결하여 간접의문문을 만드시오.

(1) Do you know?   Who met the lady?   _____

(2) Do you think?   Who met the lady?   _____

(3) Do you know?   Where does he live?   _____

(4) Do you think?   Where did he go?   _____

(5) Do you think?   When will he start?   _____

Chapter 05 관계대명사

1. This is the man **who** teaches us English.	이분이 우리에게 영어를 가르치는 분이다.
2. This is the book **which** is written by him.	이것이 그에 의해 쓰여진 그 책이다.
3. This is the first man **that** teaches us English.	이분은 우리에게 영어를 가르치는 최초의 사람이다.
4. This is **what** I want to see.	이것은 내가 보기를 원하는 것이다.

관계대명사는 글과 글을 연결하는 접속사의 역할과 대명사의 역할을 겸하는 대명사이다. 단어(형용사)가 명사를 수식할 때는 명사 앞에 놓고, 구(형용사구)가 명사를 수식할 때는 명사 뒤에 놓고, 절(형용사절)이 명사를 수식할 때는 명사 뒤에서 관계대명사로 이끄는 절을 놓는다.

- This is a **good** student.　　　　　　　(단어가 명사 수식)
- The student **in the room** is Tom.　　　(구가 명사 수식)
- This is a student **who is kind**.　　　　(문장이 명사 수식)

- This is the man. + **He** teaches us English.
　　　　　　　　　　(who)
- This is <u>the man</u> <u>who</u> <u>teaches us English</u>.
　　　선행사　관계대명사　　형용사절

선행사: 명사로서 문장(형용사절)에 의해 수식을 받는다.
관계대명사: 접속사와 대명사를 겸하는 대명사로 형용사절을 이끈다.

관계대명사의 종류와 격변화

선행사 ＼ 격	주격	소유격	목적격
사람	who	whose	whom
동물, 사물	which	whose = of which	which
사람, 동물, 사물	that	-	that
선행사 포함	what	-	what

1 who, whose, whom의 용법   선행사가 사람일 때 쓰인다.

- I know **a lady**. **She** is playing the piano.
  ➡ I know a lady **who** is playing the piano.

- **The lady** is beautiful. **She** is playing the piano.
  ➡ **The lady who** is playing the piano is beautiful.

- I know **a lady**. **Her** brother is playing baseball.
  ➡ I know **a lady whose** brother is playing baseball.

- **The lady** is beautiful. **Her** brother is playing baseball.
  ➡ **The lady whose** brother is playing baseball is beautiful.

- I know **a lady**. You met **her**.
  ➡ I know **a lady whom** you met.

- **The lady** is beautiful. You met **her**.
  ➡ **The lady whom** you met is beautiful.

2 which, of which(whose), which의 용법   선행사가 동물과 사물일 때 쓰인다.

- This is **the house**. **It** is on the hill.
  ➡ This is **the house which** is on the hill.

- **The house** is beautiful. It is on the hill.
  ➡ **The house which** is on the hill is beautiful.

- This is **the house**. **Its** roof is red.
  ➡ This is **the house whose** roof is red.
  ➡ This is **the house of which** the roof is red.
  ➡ This is **the house** the roof **of which** is red.

- This is **the house**. I found **it**.
  ➡ This is **the house which** I found.

- **The house** is beautiful. I found **it**.
  ➡ **The house which** I found is beautiful.

3 관계대명사 that의 용법 선행사가 사람, 동물, 사물일 때 쓰인다.

① 선행사로 사람과 동물(사물)이 올 때 쓰인다.
② 선행사 앞에 형용사의 최상급과 서수가 올 때 쓰인다.
③ 선행사 앞에 the only, the very, the same, all, no, -thing 등이 올 때 쓰인다.
④ 의문사가 문장 앞에 올 때 쓰인다.

· I saw the **boy** and his **dog that** were running over there.
· He is the **wisest** man **that** I know.
· This is **the first** book **that** I read.
· This is **the only** book **that** I have.
· That is **the very** man **that** I want to meet.
· This is **the same** watch **that** I lost the other day.
· This is **all** the money **that** I have.
· There is **no** man **that** doesn't love his family.
· I have **something that** I want to tell you.

관계대명사 that의 특징
❶ that의 선행사는 사람, 동물, 사물 모두가 될 수 있다.
❷ that은 who(주격), whom(목적격), which(주격, 목적격) 대신 쓰일 수 있다.
❸ that은 소유격이 없고, 또 전치사를 앞에 쓰지 못한다.
❹ that은 제한적 용법만 있고, 계속적 용법은 없다.

4 관계대명사 what의 용법 선행사를 포함하고 있으며 명사절을 이끈다.

① what은 사물에만 쓰인다.
② what은 소유격이 없다.
③ what은 제한적 용법만 있고, 계속적 용법은 없다.
④ what = the thing which = that which(~하는 것)의 뜻으로 명사절을 이끌고 주어, 목적어, 보어로 쓰인다.

· **What** she said is true.　　　　(주어)
· I believe **what** she said.　　　(목적어)
· This is **what** she said.　　　　(보어)

5 관계대명사의 주의할 점

두 문장을 관계대명사를 활용하여 한 문장으로 만들 때의 순서

❶ 두 문장에서 같은 낱말을 찾는다. (주로 명사를 선행사로, 대명사를 관계대명사로 취한다.)
❷ 대명사가 사람인지 사물인지를 찾고, 그 대명사의 격(주격, 소유격, 목적격)을 찾아서 관계대명사의 종류를 정한다.
❸ 선행사 앞에 최상급, 서수, the only 등이 있으면 that을 쓴다.
❹ 특히 주의할 점은 선행사 바로 뒤에 관계대명사가 와야 한다.
❺ 한 문장에서 대명사를 관계대명사로 뺀 후에는 그 문장의 어순은 변함이 없다.
❻ 관계대명사가 이끄는 형용사절의 해석은 '~하는, ~할, ~인' 등으로 하여 선행사인 명사를 앞에 놓아 그 명사를 수식한다.

ex 1. I know **a lady**. **She** is playing the piano.

    ⓐ a lady는 선행사로, she는 관계대명사로 정한다.
    ⓑ she는 사람이고 주격이므로 관계대명사 who를 취한다.
    ⓒ 선행사 a lady 바로 뒤에 관계대명사 who를 놓는다.
    ⓓ 이때 she를 뺀 후 나머지 낱말의 어순은 그대로 한다.

    ➡ I know **a lady who** is playing the piano. (나는 피아노를 치고 있는 한 숙녀를 안다.)

ex 2. **The lady** is beautiful. **She** is playing the piano.

    ⓐ the lady는 선행사로, she는 관계대명사로 정한다.
    ⓑ she는 사람이고 주격이므로 관계대명사 who를 취한다.
    ⓒ 선행사 the lady 바로 뒤에 관계대명사 who를 놓는다.
    ⓓ 이때 주의할 점은 beautiful 바로 뒤에 who를 놓아서는 안 된다.

    ➡ **The lady who** is playing the piano is beautiful. (피아노를 치고 있는 그 숙녀는 아름답다.)

ex 3. I know **a lady**. **Her** brother is playing baseball.

    ⓐ a lady는 선행사로, her는 관계대명사로 정한다.
    ⓑ her는 사람이고 소유격이므로 관계대명사 whose를 취한다.
    ⓒ 선행사 a lady 바로 뒤에 관계대명사 whose를 놓는다.

    ➡ I know **a lady whose** brother is playing baseball. (나는 남동생이 야구를 하고 있는 한 숙녀를 안다.)

6 관계대명사의 제한적 용법과 계속적 용법

- He has two sons **who** became doctors. (그는 의사가 된 두 아들이 있다.)
- He has two sons, **who** became doctors. (그는 두 아들이 있는데 그들은 의사가 되었다.)

1 관계대명사의 제한적 용법

① 관계대명사 앞에 콤마(,)가 없다.
② 관계대명사가 이끄는 형용사절은 선행사를 직접 수식하고 그 뜻을 제한한다.
③ 해석은 관계대명사의 뒷부분을 먼저 한다.

2 관계대명사의 계속적 용법

① 관계대명사 앞에 콤마(,)가 있다.
② 선행사를 직접 수식하지 않고 선행사를 부가적으로 설명한다.
③ 해석은 앞에서 차례로 번역해 내려간다.
④ 관계대명사의 계속적 용법은 문장의 내용에 따라서 관계대명사를 〈and, but, for, though + 대명사〉로 쓸 수 있다.

- He has two sons, **who** became doctors.
- he has two sons, **and they** became doctors.

- This is a good book, **which** is not easy.
- This is a good book, **but it** is not easy.

- I don't like the man, **who** tells a lie.
- I don't like the man, **for he** tells a lie.

- I don't know the woman, **whose** son lives near my house.
- I don't know the woman, **though her** son lives near my house.

관계대명사 that과 what은 계속적 용법으로 쓸 수 없다.
- He is the wisest man, that I know. (×)
- He is the wisest man that I know. (○)

- I don't know, what she said. (×)
- I don't know what she said. (○)

7 **〈전치사 + 관계대명사〉의 용법**   관계대명사가 전치사의 목적어일 때, 전치사는 관계대명사 앞에 놓아 도 되고 맨 뒤에 놓아도 된다.

- This is **the house**. He lives **in it**.
  ➡ This is the house **in which** he lives.
  ➡ This is the house **which** he lives **in**.

① 관계대명사의 목적격 whom과 which만이 전치사를 앞에 놓을 수 있다.
② 목적격 that 앞에는 전치사를 놓지 못하고 뒤로 돌려야 한다.
- This is the house **in that** I live. (×)
- This is the house **that I** live **in**. (○)

8 **관계대명사의 생략**   제한적 용법에서 관계대명사의 목적격은 생략할 수 있다.

① 타동사의 목적어의 경우
- This is the man **whom** I met yesterday.
  ➡ This is the man I met yesterday.

② 전치사의 목적어의 경우
- This is a chair on **which** I sit.
  ➡ This is a chair **on** I sit. (×)
  ➡ This is a chair I sit **on**. (○)

③ 〈주격관계대명사 + be동사〉를 동시에 생략할 수 있다. 단, 현재분사, 과거분사, 형용사구 앞에서만 생략된다.
- I know the baby (who is) sleeping in the room.   (현재분사 앞)
- This is the watch (which was) made in Korea.   (과거분사 앞)
- The watch (which is) on the desk is good.   (형용사구 앞)

9 **복합관계대명사**   〈관계대명사 + ever〉의 형태로 되어 있으며 선행사를 포함하고 있다. 명사절을 이끈다.

① whoever = anyone who   (~하는 사람은 누구나)
② whatever = anything that   (~하는 것은 무엇이든지)
③ whichever = any one which   (~하는 것은 어느 것이나)
- **Whoever** comes is welcome.
- Do **whatever** you like.
- You may take **whichever** you want.

10 의사관계대명사 as, but, than 등이 관계대명사 역할을 할 때 이것들을 의사관계대명사라고 한다.

1 **as가 쓰이는 경우**: 선행사 앞에 such나 the same이 오면 관계대명사 who와 which 대신에 as를 쓴다.

- I don't like a boy **who** is dishonest.　　　　　(일반 관계대명사)
- I don't like **such** a boy **as** is dishonest.　　　(의사관계대명사)
- This is **the same** watch **as** I lost yesterday.　　(같은 종류)
- This is **the same** watch **that** I lost yesterday.　(동일 물건)

2 **but이 쓰이는 경우**: but = that ~ not의 뜻으로 선행사 앞에 no, not, never 등의 부정어가 있는 경우에 쓰인다.

- There is **no** one **but** loves his country.
- There is **no** one **that** does **not** love his country.
- There is **no** rule **but** has exceptions.
- There is **no** rule **that** does **not** have exceptions.
- **Every** rule has exceptions.

▶▶ 'no ~ but ~'은 이중 부정구문이므로 긍정의 뜻을 강조하는 글이 된다.

3 **than이 쓰이는 경우**: 비교구문으로 쓰인다.

- You have **more** money **than** you need.

의문사 what과 관계대명사 what의 구별: 주절이 나타내는 내용에 따라 구별된다.

❶ **의문대명사 what의 용법**: ask, tell, doubt 등의 다음에 what이 오면 '무엇'으로 해석한다.

- She **asked** me **what** I wanted.
- She **told** me **what** she wanted.

❷ **관계대명사 what의 용법**: give, like, believe 등의 다음에 what이 오면 '것'으로 해석한다.

- She **gave** me **what** I wanted.
- She **believed what** I said.

❸ **what이 의문대명사와 관계대명사 구별 없이 다 쓰일 경우**: know, remember, forget, say 등의 동사가 오면 what이 의문대명사와 관계대명사로 쓰인다.

- She knew **what** I wanted. (의문대명사)
- She knew **what** I wanted. (관계대명사)

1. This is the man **who** wrote the book.

2. The man **who** wrote the book is my teacher.

3. This is the man **whose** son is a doctor.

4. The man **whose** son is a doctor is kind.

5. This is the woman **whom** I met in New York.

6. The woman **whom** I met the other day is gentle.

7. This is the book **which** was written by her.

8. The book **which** was written by her is interesting.

9. This is the book **whose** cover is black.

10. This is the book **of which** the cover is black.

11. This is the book the cover **of which** is black.

12. This is the book **which** I bought yesterday.

13. The book **which** I bought yesterday is interesting.

14. The boy and the book **that** I am looking for are there.

15. This is **the first** Korean **that** flew across the Pacific.

16. He is **the strongest** boy **that** I know.

17. This is **the only** friend **that** I have.

18. This is **the very** man **that** I am looking for.

19. These are **all** the books **that** I have.

20. I have **nothing that** I can give you.

Pattern Practice

21. What you need is a story.

22. I don't know **what** you want.

23. This is **what** I want.

24. They have some apples, **which** taste good.

25. He has many books, **which** he doesn't read.

26. I don't like to read these books, **which** are difficult.

27. I don't like to read these books, **which** are interesting.

28. Please give me a chair **on which** I will take a seat.

29. This is the book which I am looking **for**.

30. This is the man that I am looking **for**.

31. This is the man I am looking for.

32. This is the book I want to read.

33. This is the book written by her.

34. I saw the girl reading a book.

35. The book on the desk is mine.

36. I like **whoever** is diligent and honest.

37. You may have **whichever** you need.

38. I don't like **such** a man **as** tells a lie.

39. I made **the same** mistake **as** I had made before.

40. There are **no** parents **but** love their children.

1. 다음 두 문장을 관계대명사를 써서 한 문장으로 만드시오.

(1) This is the man.   He teaches us English.

_____

(2) This is the man.   His son is a doctor.

_____

(3) This is the man.   I met him yesterday.

_____

(4) This is the book.   It is written by him.

_____

(5) This is the book.   I bought it in Seoul.

_____

(6) This is the book.   Its cover is black.

_____

(7) The woman is happy.   She teaches us English.

_____

(8) The woman is happy.   Her son is a doctor.

_____

(9) The woman is happy.   I met her yesterday.

_____

(10) The book is good.   It is written by him.

_____

(11) The book is good.   Its cover is black.

_____

(12) The book is good.   I bought it in Seoul.

_____

(13) This is the first man.   He taught me English.

_____

(14) This is the wisest woman.   I know her.

_____

(15) This is the only money.   I have it.

_____

Part 4 대명사 Pronoun

105

2. 다음 영문을 우리말로 옮기시오.

(1) I like the student who reads many books.

_____

(2) The lady whom I met at the supermarket is my teacher.

_____

(3) This is the first Korean that has lived in Hawaii.

_____

(4) I know the boy whose father is a doctor.

_____

(5) Look at the house of which the roof is red.

_____

(6) I am looking for the book whose cover is black.

_____

(7) He bought a book which was written by a poet.

_____

(8) I lost the same watch that my father bought me last year.

_____

(9) I have no friend that I play with after school.

_____

(10) The book which was written by her is very interesting.

_____

(11) I cannot understand what you said.

_____

(12) There are no parents but love their children.

_____

(13) She has many students, who are diligent.

_____

(14) I can't read the book, which is too difficult.

_____

(15) This is the house I want to live in.

_____

3. 다음 문장을 영작하시오.

(1) 이것이 내가 좋아하는 그 책이다.

_____

(2) 이 여성분은 우리에게 영어를 가르치는 그분이다.

_____

(3) 내가 좋아하는 그 책은 쉽다.

_____

(4) 우리에게 영어를 가르치는 그분은 나의 아버지이다.

_____

(5) 이 남성분이 아들이 의사인 그 사람이다.

_____

4. 다음 (   ) 안에서 알맞은 관계대명사를 고르시오.

(1) I know the boy (who, whose, whom) name is Tom.

(2) I know the boy (who, whose, whom) is kind.

(3) I know the boy (who, whose, whom) she met.

(4) I like the book (which, whose, what) is interesting.

(5) I like the book (which, of which, whose) cover is black.

(6) I like the book (which, of which, whose) she gave me.

(7) The boy and his dog (who, which, that) are running over there look happy.

(8) This is the same watch (who, which, that) I lost.

(9) He is the first Korean (who, which, that) flew across the Pacific.

(10) This is the tallest girl (who, which, that) I know.

(11) This is the very girl (who, which, that) I want to meet.

(12) I have nothing (who, which, that) I gave you.

(13) He is the kindest man (which, that, what) I know.

(14) This is the house (that, what, whose) he lives in.

(15) This is the house in (that, what, which) he lives.

(16) The girl (whom, that, whose) studies English is my friend.

(17) The girl (who, whose, that) I like came to see me.

(18) The book (which, whose, that) cover is black is mine.

(19) There is no person (but, that, who) does not love his country.

(20) There is no rule (but, that, who) has exceptions.

5. 다음 ( ) 안에 알맞은 관계대명사를 써 넣으시오.

(1) I have a friend ( ) father is a teacher.

(2) I have a friend ( ) bought a car.

(3) I have a friend ( ) they call a Newton.

(4) I have a good friend ( ) I play with.

(5) I have a friend with ( ) I play.

(6) I have the best friend ( ) I play with.

(7) The car ( ) is made in Korean is very good.

(8) The car ( ) color is white is mine.

(9) The car ( ) he bought last year is not good.

(10) I cannot understand ( ) you said.

(11) I like ( ) is true.

(12) There is no one ( ) loves his country.

(13) There is no rule ( ) does not have exceptions.

(14) ( ) he said so is true.

(15) This is the same watch ( ) I lost the other day.

(16) I don't like such a boy ( ) tells a lie.

(17) I know the boy and his dog ( ) are running over there.

(18) The man ( ) is happy is not always rich.

(19) The house ( ) he lives in is very beautiful.

(20) The house in ( ) I live is very beautiful.

관계부사

P · r · e · v · i · e · w

1. This is the house **where** I live.	이것이 내가 사는 집이다.
2. It is time **when** I must start.	내가 떠나야 할 시간이다.
3. This is the reason **why** I was late.	이것이 내가 늦은 이유이다.
4. This is (the way) **how** I cook.	이것이 내가 요리하는 방법이다.

관계부사는 글과 글을 연결하는 접속사와 부사의 역할을 하고, 선행사를 수식하는 형용사절을 이끈다. 선행사는 장소, 시간, 이유, 방법을 나타내는 명사이다.

〈관계부사 = 전치사 + 관계대명사〉의 관계가 있다. 즉 〈where = in which〉이다.

관계부사의 종류

용도	선행사	관계부사	관계부사 = (전치사 + 관계대명사)
장소	the place	where	where = in which
시간	the time	when	when = on(at) which
이유	the reason	why	why = for which
방법	(the way)	how	how = in which

1 where의 용법   선행사가 '장소'일 때 쓰인다.

· This is **the house**. I live **there**. (there = in it)

⇒ This is **the house** and I live in it.

⇒ This is **the house where** I live.　　　　　(관계부사)

⇒ This is **the house in which** I live.　　　　(전치사 + 관계대명사)

⇒ This is **the house which** I live **in**.

⇒ This is **the house** I live **in**.　　　　　　(관계대명사 생략)

2 when의 용법 선행사가 '시간'일 때 쓰인다.

· I don't know **the day**. She started **on the day**.
  ➡ I don't know **the day when** she started.　　　(관계부사)
  ➡ I don't know **the day on which** she started.　　(전치사 + 관계대명사)
  ➡ I don't know **the day which** she started **on**.
  ➡ I don't know **the day** she started **on**.　　　(관계대명사 생략)

3 why의 용법 선행사가 '이유'일 때 쓰인다.

· This is **the reason**. He was late **for the reason**.
  ➡ This is **the reason why** he was late.　　　(관계부사)
  ➡ This is **the reason for which** he was late.　　(전치사 + 관계대명사)
  ➡ This is **the reason which** he was late **for**.
  ➡ This is **the reason** he was late **for**.　　　(관계대명사 생략)

  ▶▶ why의 선행사는 the reason만이다.

4 how의 용법 선행사가 '방법'일 때 쓰인다.

· Tell me **the way**. You made it in the way.
  ➡ Tell me **the way** you made it.　　　(관계부사)
  ➡ Tell me **how** you made it.　　　(관계부사)
  ➡ Tell me **the way that** you made it.　　(관계대명사)
  ➡ Tell me **the way in which** you made it.　　(전치사 + 관계대명사)

  ▶▶ 현대 영어에서는 the way how는 잘 쓰이지 않으므로 the way나 how만을 쓰든지, the way that 혹은 the way in which를 쓴다.

5 관계부사의 제한적 용법과 계속적 용법

· This is the town **where** I was born. (이곳은 내가 태어난 도시이다.)
· I went to the town, **where** I stayed for a week.
  (나는 그 도시에 갔다, 그런데 거기서 나는 일주일 동안 머물렀다.)

1 관계부사의 제한적 용법
  ① 관계부사 앞에 콤마(,)가 없다.
  ② 관계부사는 형용사절을 이끌고 선행사를 수식한다.
  ③ 해석은 관계부사 뒷부분부터 먼저 한다.

2 **관계부사의 계속적 용법**

① 관계부사 앞에 콤마(,)가 있다.

② 관계부사는 〈접속사 + 부사〉로 바꾸어 쓸 수 있다.

③ 해석은 앞부분부터 내려서 한다.

where = and there, when = and then으로 쓰인다.

· I went to America, **where** I met Mr. Brown.

= I went to America, **and there** I met Mr. Brown.

· I went to church yesterday, **when** I met Mr. Brown.

= I went to church yesterday, **and then** I met Mr. Brown.

6 **관계부사의 선행사 생략**   관계부사의 선행사를 생략하면 형용사절이 명사절로 된다.

· This is just the time **when** I must get up.   (형용사절)
· This is just **when** I must get up.   (명사절)

· This is the place **where** he was born.   (형용사절)
· This is **where** he was born.   (명사절)

· This is the reason **why** I don't like you.   (형용사절)
· This is **why** I don't like you.   (명사절)

· This is the way **that** I drive a car.   (형용사절)
· This is **the way** I drive a car.   (형용사절)
· This is **how** I drive a car.   (명사절)

7 **복합관계부사**   〈관계부사 + ever〉의 형태로 되어 있으며, 선행사를 포함하고 있다. 부사절을 이끈다.

① wherever = at any place where (어디든지)

② whenever = at any time when (언제든지)

③ however = no matter how (아무리 ~하더라도)

· **Wherever** you go, you will not forget me.

· **Whenever** you see me, you will be happy.

· **However** hard you may try, you cannot finish it.

1. This is the village **where** he was born.

2. This is the village **in which** he was born.

3. This is the village **which** he was born **in**.

4. I remember the day **when** I met you.

5. I remember the day **on which** I met you.

6. I remember the day **which** I met you **on**.

7. I know the reason **why** she left here.

8. I know the reason **for which** she left here.

9. I know the reason **which** she left here **for**.

10. I don't like the way **that** you succeed.

11. I don't like **the way** you succeed.

12. I don't like **how** you succeed.

13. I don't like the way **in which** you succeed.

14. This is the city **where** I have lived for ten years.

15. I went to the city, **where** I stayed for two weeks.

16. I went to the city, **and there** I stayed for two weeks.

17. I went to the city, **and** I stayed **there** for two weeks.

18. My birthday is the day **when** my mother was also born into the world.

19. My birthday is July 25, **when** my mother was also born into the world.

20. My birthday is July 25, **and then** my mother was also born into the world.

종합문제

1. 다음 영문을 우리말로 옮기시오.

(1) This is the village where I was born. _____

(2) This is Busan, where I was born. _____

(3) This is the village in which I was born. _____

(4) Today is the day when I was born. _____

(5) Today is September 16, when I was born. _____

(6) This is the reason why I don't like you. _____

(7) This is the way that I made the house. _____

2. 다음 문장을 영작하시오.

(1) 너는 그녀가 태어난 집을 아니? _____

(2) 나는 너에게 어제 내가 결석한 이유를 말할 수 없다. _____

(3) 당신이 서울을 떠나는 날을 나에게 말해줄 수 있습니까? _____

3. 다음 두 문장의 뜻이 같도록 ( ) 안에 알맞은 말을 써 넣어라.

(1) I went to New York, where I stayed for a week.

I went to New York, ( ) ( ) I stayed for a week.

(2) My birthday is July 25, when my mother was also born into the world.

My birthday is July 25, ( ) ( ) my mother was also born into the world.

(3) There are many places where we play baseball.

There are many places ( ) ( ) we play baseball.

(4) There is no reason why you must get up early.

There is no reason ( ) ( ) you must get up early.

(5) I know the year when she was born.

I know the year ( ) ( ) she was born.

4. 다음 ( ) 안에 알맞은 관계대명사와 관계부사를 써 넣어라.

1. The house ( ) I live in is beautiful.

2. The house ( ) I was born is beautiful.

3. This is ( ) I was looking for two weeks.

4. This is the girl with ( ) he has played.

5. This is the way ( ) he studied English.

Part 4 대명사 Pronoun

113

Part 5

형용사

ADJECTIVE

형용사의 종류

P·r·e·v·i·e·w

1. **This** book is easier than **that** one.	이 책은 저 책보다 더 쉽다.
2. He is a **kind** man.	그는 친절한 사람이다.
3. The boy has **a few** books in his room.	그 소년은 자기 방에 약간의 책을 가지고 있다.

형용사는 명사를 수식하는 말로 대명형용사, 성질형용사, 수량형용사 3종류가 있다.

1 대명형용사 대명사가 명사 앞에서 형용사로 쓰인다.

① 지시형용사: **this** book, **that** boy, **these** books 등
② 소유형용사: **my** house, **his** friend, **her** school 등
③ 의문형용사: **what** book, **which** pencil 등
④ 부정형용사: **some** water, **any** books, **all** men 등

2 성질형용사 사람이나 사물의 성질, 상태를 나타내는 형용사이다.

① 원래의 형용사: a **pretty** girl, a **good** book 등
② 고유명사에서 온 것: an **English** boy, a **French** girl 등
③ 물질명사에서 온 것: a **silver** spoon, a **gold** watch 등
④ 분사에서 온 것: a **sleeping** baby, a **used** car 등

3 수량형용사 수, 양, 정도를 나타내는 형용사이다.

① 수사: 일정한 수를 나타내는 말이다.
 • 기수: one, two, three, four 등
 • 서수: first, second, third, fourth 등
 • 배수: half, double, twice, three times 등
② 부정 수량형용사: 일정하지 않은 수량을 나타낸다.
 • few, little, many, much, some 등

TIP

명사에 어미를 붙여 형용사가 된 것

sun - sunny (햇빛 나는)	man - manly (남자다운)
rain - rainy (비 오는)	love - lovely (사랑스러운)
cloud - cloudy (흐린)	fool - foolish (어리석은)

Chapter 02

형용사의 용법

P·r·e·v·i·e·w

1. This is a **beautiful** lady. (한정적 용법)
2. This lady is **beautiful**. (서술적 용법)
3. I think this lady **beautiful**. (서술적 용법)
4. I want to see something **beautiful**. (한정적 용법)

이 분은 아름다운 숙녀이다.
이 숙녀는 아름답다.
나는 이 숙녀가 아름답다고 생각한다.
나는 아름다운 것 보기를 원한다.

1 한정적 용법   형용사가 명사와 대명사의 앞 또는 뒤에서 직접 그것을 수식한다.

- He is a **good** student.   (명사 수식)
- My birthday party will be a **big** one.   (대명사 수식)
- I want something **white**.   (부정대명사 수식)
- Seoul has many houses, **small and large**.   (대조되는 형용사)

> **한정적 용법으로만 쓰이는 형용사**
> - wooden, woolen, golden, silken처럼 −en으로 끝나는 형용사
> - elder, former, latter, inner처럼 −er로 끝나는 형용사
> - only(유일한), total(총), mere(단순한) 등

2 서술적 용법   형용사가 주격보어와 목적격보어로 쓰인다.

- She is **happy**.   (주격보어)
- I think her **happy**.   (목적격보어)

> - afraid, asleep, alive, awake, aware처럼 a−로 시작되는 형용사
> - well, fond, glad, sorry 등의 형용사

3 한정적 용법과 서술적 용법으로 쓰일 때 뜻이 달라지는 형용사

- A **certain** man came to see you.   (한정적 용법)
- I am **certain** that he will come to see you.   (서술적 용법)

- The **late** Mr. Brown was a famous scholar.   (한정적 용법)
- Mr. Brown was **late** yesterday.   (서술적 용법)

Pattern Practice

1. This is a **beautiful** flower.

2. This flower is **beautiful**.

3. **What** do you want to have?

4. **What** book do you want to have?

5. Are there **any** trees in the garden?

6. There is **some** milk in the glass.

7. Are these **your books**? Yes, they are **mine**.

8. He looks like English.

9. He is **not** an English boy, **but** an American boy.

10. This is a **white** house.

11. This house is **white**.

12. I want to have something **white**.

13. There are many houses **small** and **large** on the hill.

14. My family lives in a **wooden** house.

15. His grandmother is still **alive**.

16. I am **fond** of music very much.

17. I am **glad** to see you.

18. The **late** President Lincoln was a **great** man in American history.

19. My brother **is** always **late for** school.

20. It **rains** today. It is **rainy** today.

1. 다음 영문을 우리말로 옮기시오.

(1) What does she want to read? _____

(2) What book does she want to read? _____

(3) This is a happy girl. _____

(4) This girl is very happy. _____

(5) I made this girl happy. _____

(6) He loves a lovely girl. _____

(7) How foolish she is! _____

(8) My father's birthday party was a big one. _____

(9) He has taught the blind and the deaf for ten years. _____

(10) The present queen of England is Elizabeth. _____

(11) The Queen Elizabeth is present at the meeting. _____

(12) My sister is afraid of a dog. _____

(13) I want to drink something cold. _____

(14) It was a very exciting game. _____

(15) Everybody was much excited to see the game. _____

2. 다음 문장을 영작하시오.

(1) 그녀는 아름다운 소녀이다. _____

(2) 그 소녀는 아름답다. _____

(3) 나는 그 소녀가 아름답다고 생각한다. _____

(4) 나는 아름다운 것을 보기를 원한다. _____

(5) 그 소녀는 약간의 책을 가지고 있다. _____

형용사의 위치

1. **Those two old** men went to the mountain.
2. **All** the boys are diligent.
3. I want to have something **cold**.

저 두 노인들이 산에 갔다.
모든 소년들은 부지런하다.
나는 찬 것 먹기를 원한다.

1 형용사의 일반적인 어순 〈관사 + 부사 + 형용사 + 명사〉이다.

· She is a very good student.
· They are very good students.
· They are the very good students.

2 두 개 이상의 다른 형용사가 한 명사를 수식하는 경우 〈관사(대명형용사) + 수량형용사 + 성질형용사 + 명사〉의 어순이다.

· **The two old** men came here yesterday.
· **These two old** men went to the park.
· **My two kind** friends came to meet me.

3 형용사가 명사 뒤에 오는 경우

① something, nothing, anything, everything 등을 수식하는 형용사는 그 뒤에 온다.
   · I want to eat something **cold**.
   · Do you want to eat anything **hot**?

② 형용사에 수식어가 붙어 있을 때
   · Korea is a **famous** country.
   · Korea is a country **famous** for a fast internet connection.

the + 형용사 = 복수 보통명사
· The rich are not always happy.
· The old have nothing to do.

수량형용사

	기수		서수		기수		서수
1	one	1st	first	11	eleven	11th	eleventh
2	two	2nd	second	12	twelve	12th	twelfth
3	three	3rd	third	13	thirteen	13th	thirteenth
4	four	4th	fourth	14	fourteen	14th	fourteenth
5	five	5th	fifth	15	fifteen	15th	fifteenth
6	six	6th	sixth	16	sixteen	16th	sixteenth
7	seven	7th	seventh	17	seventeen	17th	seventeenth
8	eight	8th	eighth	18	eighteen	18th	eighteenth
9	nine	9th	ninth	19	nineteen	19th	nineteenth
10	ten	10th	tenth	20	twenty	20th	twentieth
21	twenty-one	21st	twenty-first	31	thirty-one	31st	thirty-first
22	twenty-two	22nd	twenty-second	41	forty-one	41st	forty-first
23	twenty-three	23rd	twenty-third	51	fifty-one	51st	fifty-first
24	twenty-four	24th	twenty-fourth	61	sixty-one	61st	sixty-first
25	twenty-five	25th	twenty-fifth	71	seventy-one	71st	seventy-first
30	thirty	30th	thirtieth				
40	forty	40th	fortieth				
50	fifty	50th	fiftieth				
60	sixty	60th	sixtieth				
70	seventy	70th	seventieth				
80	eighty	80th	eightieth				
90	ninety	90th	ninetieth				
100	one hundred	100th	one hundredth				
101	one hudred (and) one						
1000	one thousand	1000th	one thousandth				

Part 5 형용사 Adjective

숫자 읽는 법

1 정수

- 200 = two hundred
- 2,000 = two thousand
- 20,000 = twenty thousand
- 123,456,789 = one hundred (and) twenty-three million, four hundred (and) fifty-six thousand, seven hundred eighty-nine

미국에서는 hundred 다음에 and를 보통 생략한다.
hundred, thousand, million, billion 다음에 's'를 붙이지 않는다.
단, 막연히 수백, 수천, 수백만 등을 읽을 때 's'를 붙인다.
ex. hundreds, thousands, millions 등

2 분수와 소수

- $\frac{1}{2}$ = a half (= one half)
- $2\frac{1}{2}$ = two and a half
- $\frac{1}{3}$ = a third (= one third)
- $\frac{2}{3}$ = two-thirds
- $\frac{1}{4}$ = a quarter
- $\frac{3}{4}$ = three-fourths (= three quarters)

분자는 기수로, 분모는 서수로 읽는다. 분자가 2 이상인 경우에는 분모에 's'를 붙여 읽는다.
- 3.14 = three point one four

3 연호, 월일, 시간

1 연호: 연호는 보통 두 자리씩 나누어 읽는다.
- 1999: nineteen ninety-nine
- 1900: nineteen hundred
- 2006: twenty [ou] six = twenty hundred (and) six

2 월일
- 9월 16일: September (the) 16th = the 16th of September
- 3월 17일: March (the) 17th = the 17th of March

3 **시간**

- 9시 30분(오전): 9:30 a.m. = nine thirty (= half past nine)
- 2시 15분(오후): 2:15 p.m. = two fifteen (= a quarter past two)
- 1시 20분(오후): 1:20 p.m. = one twenty (= twenty past one)
- 1시 55분(오후): 1:55 p.m. = one fifty−five (= five to two) = fifty−five past one

4 전화번호, 화폐, 방, 호수

1 **전화번호**: 하나씩 순서대로 읽고, 0은 [ou]로 읽는다.

- 855−6343 : eight five five six three four three
- 857−5069 : eight five seven five [ou] six nine

2 **화폐**: $3.20 = three dollars (and) twenty (cents)

3 **방 호수**: Room 707 = room seven [ou] seven

부정수량형용사

P·r·e·v·i·e·w

1. We have **many** books.	우리는 많은 책을 가지고 있다.
2. We have **much** rain in summer.	여름에 비가 많이 온다.
3. I have **a few** friends.	나는 약간의 친구가 있다.
4. I have **a little** money.	나는 약간의 돈이 있다.

1 many와 much의 용법

① many는 셀 수 있는 복수명사 앞에, 즉 수를 나타내는 명사 앞에 쓰인다.

② much는 셀 수 없는 단수명사 앞에, 즉 양을 나타내는 명사 앞에 쓰인다.
- There are **many** students in the class.
- There is **much** water in the pool.
- How **many** books do you have?
- How **much** money do you have?

③ a lot of(=lots of)는 many(수)와 much(양)에 둘 다 쓰인다. 단, 긍정문에서만 a lot of가 many, much 대신에 쓰이고, 의문문과 부정문에서는 항상 many, much를 쓴다.
- I have **a lot of** books. (긍정문)
- I don't have **many** books. (부정문)
- Do you have **many** books? (의문문)
- I have **a lot of** money. (긍정문)
- I don't have **much** money. (부정문)
- Do you have **much** money? (의문문)

2 a few와 a little의 용법

① a few와 few는 셀 수 있는 복수명사 앞에 쓰이고, a little과 little은 셀 수 없는 단수명사 앞에 쓰인다.

② few와 little은 '거의 없는'의 뜻으로 부정적 의미를 가지고 있다. a few와 a little은 '조금 있는'의 뜻으로 긍정적 의미를 가지고 있다.

③ not a few = many와 not a little = much는 '적지 않은'의 뜻이다.
- There are **a few** students in the class.
- There are **few** students in the class.

- There is **a little** milk in the glass.
- There is **little** milk in the glass.

124

- **A few** boys are playing baseball on the playground.
- **Few** boys are playing baseball on the playground.

- **A little** water is left in the glass.
- **Little** water is left in the glass.

- **Not a few** students passed the examination.
- **Not a little** money was spent by him.

TIP

Korea: 한국	Korean: 한국어, 한국의, 한국인
America: 미국	American: 미국어, 미국의, 미국인
England: 영국	English: 영어, 영국의, 영국인(=Englishman)
France: 프랑스	French: 프랑스어, 프랑스의, 프랑스인(=Frenchman)
Japan: 일본	Japanese: 일본어, 일본의, 일본인
China: 중국	Chinese: 중국어, 중국의, 중국인
Russia: 러시아	Russian: 러시아어, 러시아의, 러시아인
Spain: 스페인	Spanish: 스페인어, 스페인의, 스페인인
Germany: 독일	German: 독일어, 독일의, 독일인
Greece: 그리스	Greek: 그리스어, 그리스의, 그리스인
Switzerland: 스위스	Swiss: 스위스어, 스위스의, 스위스인
The Netherlands: 네덜란드	Dutch: 네덜란드어, 네덜란드의, 네덜란드인

형용사의 비교

P·r·e·v·i·e·w

1. He is **tall**. (원급)	그는 키가 크다.
2. He is **taller** than I. (비교급)	그는 나보다 키가 더 크다.
3. He is the **tallest** student in the class. (최상급)	그는 반에서 키가 가장 큰 학생이다.

형용사는 명사의 성질, 수량, 상태 등을 다른 것과 비교하여 그 정도를 나타내기 위해 원급, 비교급, 최상급의 3가지 어형 변화가 있다.

1 형용사의 비교급, 최상급 만드는 방법

1 규칙 변화

① 원급의 어미에 −er, −est를 붙여 비교급, 최상급을 만든다. (1음절 형용사와 2음절 형용사의 일부)

ⓐ 원급의 어미에 −er, −est를 붙인다.

원급	비교급	최상급
tall	taller	tallest
old	older	oldest

ⓑ −e로 끝나면 −r, −st를 붙인다.

원급	비교급	최상급
wise	wiser	wisest
large	larger	largest

ⓒ 〈자음 + y〉로 끝나면 y를 i로 고쳐 −er, −est를 붙인다.

원급	비교급	최상급
easy	easier	easiest
happy	happier	happiest

ⓓ 〈단모음 + 자음〉으로 끝나면 자음 하나를 더 겹쳐 쓰고 −er, −est를 붙인다.

원급	비교급	최상급
big	bigger	biggest
hot	hotter	hottest

ⓔ 2음절 형용사의 어미가 −er, −y, −(l)y, −ow, −le, −some 등으로 끝나면 −er, −est를 붙인다.

원급	비교급	최상급
clever	cleverer	cleverest
pretty	prettier	prettiest
early	earlier	earliest
narrow	narrower	narrowest
idle	idler	idlest
handsome	handsomer	handsomest

② 3음절 이상의 형용사와 2음절 형용사 일부는 more, most를 붙인다.

원급	비교급	최상급
beautiful	more beautiful	most beautiful
diligent	more diligent	most diligent

③ 2음절의 형용사로 어미가 −ous, −ful, −ing, −less, −ive 등으로 끝나면 more, most를 붙인다.

원급	비교급	최상급
famous	more famous	most famous
useful	more useful	most useful
useless	more useless	most useless

2 불규칙 변화

원급	비교급	최상급
good well	better	best
bad ill	worse	worst
many much	more	most
little	less	least
old	older elder	oldest (나이관계) eldest (형제관계)
late	later latter	latest (시간) last (순서)
far	farther further	farthest (거리) furthest (정도)

Pattern Practice

1. She is a very **good** teacher.

2. The very **good** books are my teacher's.

3. These two **old** men are very wise.

4. My two **pretty** sisters are playing the violin.

5. The English are **kind** and **polite**.

6. He was **born** on September 16th, 2010.

7. There are **many** books in the library.

8. There are **many** people in Seoul.

9. There is **much** water in the pool.

10. She has **a few** friends in America.

11. She has **few** friends in Seoul.

12. He has **a little** money in his purse.

13. He has **little** money in his purse.

14. Not **a few** people think so.

15. He has not **a little** money in his purse.

16. He has **a lot of** books in his library.

17. He has **a lot of** money in the bank.

18. He likes her **a lot**.

19. **Few** people believe what he said.

20. We have **lots of** snow in winter.

연습문제

1. 다음 명사의 형용사형을 쓰시오.

(1) sun ( )   (6) love ( )

(2) friend ( )   (7) fool ( )

(3) cloud ( )   (8) rain ( )

(4) England ( )   (9) France ( )

(5) Korea ( )   (10) Japan ( )

2. 다음 ( ) 안에 형용사의 비교급과 최상급을 써 넣으시오.

원급	비교급	최상급	원급	비교급	최상급
(1) good (	) (	)	(6) little (	) (	)
(2) big (	) (	)	(7) famous (	) (	)
(3) clever (	) (	)	(8) large (	) (	)
(4) much (	) (	)	(9) old (	) (	)
(5) pretty (	) (	)	(10) bad (	) (	)

3. 다음 숫자를 영어로 쓰시오.

(1) 2 (기수):   (11) 2 (서수):   (21) 82 (기수):

(2) 12 (기수):   (12) 12 (서수):   (22) 82 (서수):

(3) 20 (기수):   (13) 20 (서수):   (23) 9 (기수):

(4) 4 (기수):   (14) 4 (서수):   (24) 9 (서수):

(5) 14 (기수):   (15) 14 (서수):   (25) 19 (기수):

(6) 40 (기수):   (16) 40 (서수):   (26) 19 (서수):

(7) 5 (기수):   (17) 5 (서수):   (27) 100 (기수):

(8) 15 (기수):   (18) 15 (서수):   (28) 100 (서수):

(9) 50 (기수):   (19) 50 (서수):   (29) 1000 (기수):

(10) 31 (기수):   (20) 31 (서수):   (30) 321, 654, 987 (기수):

4. 다음을 영어로 쓰시오.

(1) $\frac{1}{2}$:   (5) $\frac{3}{4}$:

(2) 1999년: (6) 1906년:

(3) 9월 16일: (7) 3.14:

(4) 855-5052:   (8) 2:15 p.m.:

Part 5 형용사 Adjective

129

5. 다음 ( ) 안에서 알맞은 것을 고르시오.

(1) I have (many, much) books in the library.

(2) We have (many, much) rain in summer.

(3) He has (a few, a little) money in the purse.

(4) He has (a few, a little) apples in the box.

(5) I have (much, a lot of) balls in my house.

(6) I don't have (much, a lot of) money in my purse.

(7) Do you have (many, a lot of) books in your house?

(8) She has (many, a lot of) coffee.

(9) There are (few, little) students in the class.

(10) There is (few, little) water in the pool.

6. 다음 ( ) 안에서 알맞은 것을 고르시오.

(1) The rich (are, is) not always happy.

(2) The beautiful (are, is) true.

(3) The game is (exciting, excited).

(4) Her grandmother was (alive, lived) in 2018.

(5) I have (a little, little) money. If I have (a little, little), I can lend you some.

7, 다음 문장에서 잘못된 곳을 바르게 고치시오.

(1) I know a asleep baby well. _____

(2) Two my kind friends came here. _____

(3) I want to drink cold something. _____

(4) Look at two the good students. _____

(5) He is pleasant to come home early. _____

2 원급의 용법   형용사의 원급을 사용하여 정도를 나타내는 비교의 형식이다.

① 〈as + 원급 + as〉: ~만큼 ~하다   (동등비교)
  · He is **as** young **as** I.
  · She is **as** beautiful **as** my mother.
  · He can run **as** fast **as** I.

② 〈not so + 원급 + as〉: ~만큼 ~하지 않다 (동등비교)
  · She is **not so** young **as** I.
  · She is **not so** beautiful **as** my mother.
  · He can **not** run **as** fast **as** I.

    ▶▶ 구어체에서는 not as ~ as를 보통 사용한다.

③ 〈times as + 원급 + as〉: ~배 ~하다   (배수비교)
  · This house is three **times as** large **as** that one.
    = This house is three times **larger than** that one.
  · This pencil is **twice as** long **as** that one.

원급의 주의할 용법

❶ as ~ as possible / as ~ as one can: 가능한 한 ~
❷ as good as: ~와 다름없는
❸ as many as: ~만큼이나
❹ so much as: ~조차도(= even)

  · You had better run **as** fast **as possible**.
  · He is **as good as** dead.
  · I have **as many as** one thousand books.
  · He left without **so much as** saying good-bye.

3 비교급의 용법   두 가지의 성질, 상태, 수량을 비교하는 형식이다.

① 〈비교급 + than〉: ~보다 더 ~한   (우등비교)
  · He is **younger than** I.
  · He is **older than** I by two years.
    = He is two years **older than** I.
  · My mother is **more** beautiful **than** she.

② 〈less + 원급 + than〉: ~보다 덜 ~하다   (열등비교)
  · He is **less** young **than** I.
  · She is **less** old **than** I.
  · She is **less** beautiful **than** my mother.

③ superior to: than 대신에 to를 쓴다.

- superior to: ~보다 월등한
- inferior to: ~보다 못한
- senior to: ~보다 손위의
- junior to: ~보다 어린
- prefer A to B(= A better than B): B보다 A를 더 좋아하다

- He is **superior to** me in music.
- She is **inferior to** my sister in playing the piano.
- He is **senior to** me.
- He is **junior to** me.
- I **prefer** America **to** Russia.
  = I like America **better than** Russia.

비교급의 주의할 용법

❶ 〈the + 비교급 + of the two〉: 둘 중에서 더 ~한
비교급의 형용사 뒤에 'of the two'가 오면 비교급 앞에 정관사 the를 쓴다.
- He is **the taller of the two**.
- She is **the older of the two**.

❷ 〈Which ~ + 비교급, A or B?〉: A와 B 중에서 어느 쪽이 ~인가
- Which is **larger**, the sun **or** the moon?
- Which do you like **better**, coffee **or** milk?

❸ 〈the + 비교급 ~, the + 비교급 ~〉: ~하면 할수록, 더욱 ~하다.
- **The more** we have, **the more** we want.
- **The higher** we go up, **the colder** it becomes.
- **The sooner, the better.**(= **The sooner** it is, **the better** it will be.)

❹ 비교급의 강조: much, far, even, still, yet 등은 비교급을 강조하는 어구로 '훨씬, 한층'의 뜻으로 쓰인다.
- He is **much** taller than I.
- The sun is **far** larger than the moon.

❺ no more than = only: 겨우 ~뿐, 단지 ~만
no less than = as many(much) as: ~만큼이나
- She has **no more than** 10 books.
  = She has **only** 10 books.

- She has **no less than** 1,000 books.
  = She has **as many as** 1,000 books.

- He has **no less than** 10 dollars.
- He has **as much as** 10 dollars.

not more than = at most: 기껏해야
not less than = at least: 적어도
- He has **not more than** 10 dollars.
- He has **not less than** 10 dollars.

❻ A is no more B than C is D: A가 B가 아닌 것은 C가 D가 아닌 것과 같다
- A whale is **no more** a fish **than** a horse is.
  = A whale is **not** a fish **any more than** a horse is.

❼ 비교급 + and + 비교급: 점점 ~하다
- It is getting **warmer and warmer** in these days.
- It is getting **darker and darker**.

4 최상급의 용법   셋 이상의 것 중에서 '가장 ~하다'라는 뜻이다.

① 〈the + 최상급 + of + 복수명사〉: ~ 중에서 가장 ~하다
  〈the + 최상급 + in + 장소, 집단〉: ~에서 가장 ~하다
- Tom is **the tallest** of the boys.
- He is **the oldest** of three boys.
- Tom is **the tallest** boy in our class.
- She is **the most** beautiful girl in her family.

② 형용사의 최상급에는 정관사 the를 붙이지만, 부사의 최상급에는 the를 안 붙인다.
- I get up **earliest** in the family.
- Carl Lewis runs **fastest** in the world.
- Tom can run **fastest** of the three.

최상급의 주의할 용법

❶ a most(= a very): 매우, the most: 가장 ~, most: 대부분의
- This is **a most** beautiful flower.
- This is **the most** beautiful flower.
- **Most** flowers are beautiful.

❷ 최상급의 뜻을 나타내는 여러 가지 표현으로 최상급, 원급, 비교급 등이 있다.
- He is **the tallest** boy in the class.   (최상급)
  = No other boy in the class is as **tall** as he.   (원급)
  = No other boy in the class is **taller than** he.   (비교급)
  = He is **taller than** any other boy in the class.   (비교급)
  = He is **the tallest** of all the boys in the class.   (최상급)

Pattern Practice

1. She is **as** beautiful **as** my sister.

2. She is **not so** beautiful **as** my sister.

3. She is **more** beautiful **than** my sister.

4. She is not **more** beautiful **than** my sister.

5. She is **less** beautiful **than** my sister.

6. She is **the most** beautiful of them.

7. She is **the most** beautiful in her family.

8. She can run **fastest** in her class.

9. Which do you like **better**, coffee or milk?

10. Which do you like **best**, an apple, an orange or a banana?

11. Tom is **the tallest** boy in his class.

12. Tom is **the taller** of the two.

13. He is **older than** I.

14. He is my **elder** brother.

15. Mr. Kim came here **latest**.

16. Miss Kim arrived **last**.

17. Tom is three years **older than** Jack.

18. Tom is **older than** Jack by three years.

19. This river is three times **wider than** that one.

20. This river is three times **as** wide **as** that one.

21. This book is **superior to** that one.

22. This book is **better than** that one.

23. My English is **inferior to** your English.

24. My English is **worse than** your English.

25. I like him **better than** her.

26. I like him **better than** she.

27. I **prefer** apples **to** bananas.

28. I like apples **better than** bananas.

29. It grew **colder and colder**.

30. **The more** we learn, **the wiser** we become.

31. I have **no more than** one hundred won.

32. I have **not more than** one hundred won.

33. I have **no less than** one hundred won.

34. I have **not less than** one hundred won.

35. I am **no more** kind **than** you are.

36. Mt. Everest is **the highest** mountain in the world.

37. No other mountain in the world is **as** high **as** Mt. Everest.

38. No other mountain in the world is **higher than** Mt. Everest.

39. Mt. Everest is **higher than** any other mountain in the world.

40. Mt. Everest is **the highest** of all the mountains in the world.

1. 다음 영문을 우리말로 옮기시오.

(1) He is as strong as I.

_____

(2) He is not so strong as my brother.

_____

(3) He is stronger than I.

_____

(4) The lady is more beautiful than my sister.

_____

(5) The lady is less beautiful than my mother.

_____

(6) He has as many books as I.

_____

(7) He is the strongest boy in his class.

_____

(8) Which do you like better, coffee or milk?

_____

(9) Jack is the taller of the two.

_____

(10) Jack is two years older than Tom.

_____

(11) This pencil is three times as long as that one.

_____

(12) The higher we go up, the colder it becomes.

_____

(13) I prefer coffee to milk.

_____

(14) I like you better than her.

_____

(15) I like you better than she.

_____

(16) I have no more than ten dollars.

_____

(17) It is getting warmer and warmer.

_____

(18) I have no less than ten dollars.

_____

(19) Tom is taller than any other boy in the class.

_____

(20) Tom is the tallest boy in the class.

_____

2. 다음 ( ) 안에서 알맞은 것을 고르시오.

(1) The boy is (older, elder) than Tom.

(2) The girl is my (older, elder) sister.

(3) Tom is the (tallest, taller) of the two.

(4) Jack is the (oldest, older) boy of his friends.

(5) Tom likes history better (to, than) science.

(6) Tom prefer history (to, than) science.

(7) He is as (young, younger) as I.

(8) He is (young, younger) than I.

(9) She is the wisest (of, in) her class.

(10) He is the tallest (of, in) all the boys.

(11) She is (clever, cleverer) than you.

(12) This book is (more, better) than that one.

(13) She has (more, better) money than you.

(14) The party is (more, much) bigger than that one.

(15) The higher we go up, the (cold, colder) it becomes.

3. 다음 두 문장의 내용이 같아지도록 ( ) 안에 알맞은 말을 써 넣으시오.

(1) Jane is not so tall as Mary.

Jane is ( ) tall than Mary.

(2) This is a most interesting book.

This is a ( ) interesting book.

(3) He has no more than ten dollars.

He has ( ) ten dollars.

(4) He has not more than a thousand won.

He has at ( ) a thousand won.

(5) Seoul is the largest city in Korea.

Seoul is larger than any ( ) city in Korea.

4. 다음 문장의 내용과 같아지도록 (   ) 안에 알맞은 말을 써 넣으시오.

New York is the largest city in America.

(1) New York is larger than (   ) (   ) city in America.
(2) No other city in America is (   ) large as New York.
(3) No other city in America is (   ) than New York.
(4) New York is the largest (   ) (   ) the cities in America.

5. 다음 문장의 밑줄 친 부분을 구별하여 우리말로 옮기시오.

(1) This is <u>a most</u> beautiful flower. _____

(2) This is <u>the most</u> beautiful flower. _____

(3) <u>Most</u> flowers are beautiful. _____

(4) She has <u>no more than</u> ten dollars. _____

(5) She has <u>no less than</u> ten dollars. _____

(6) She has <u>not more than</u> ten dollars. _____

(7) She has <u>not less than</u> ten dollars. _____

(8) He <u>is superior to</u> me in history. _____

(9) He <u>is inferior to</u> me in science. _____

(10) He is <u>as good as</u> dead. _____

6. 다음 영문을 우리말로 옮기시오.

(1) 그는 나만큼 키가 크다. _____

(2) 그는 나보다 키가 크다. _____

(3) 그녀는 나만큼 예쁘지 않다. _____

(4) 그녀는 그녀의 반에서 가장 키가 큰 소녀이다. _____

(5) 그녀는 그들 중에서 가장 아름다운 숙녀이다. _____

종합문제

1 다음 ( ) 안에서 알맞은 것을 고르시오.

(1) I like him better than (she, her).

(2) I am taller than (she, her).

(3) I have three times (as, as many) books as he has.

(4) He has three times (as, as much) money as I have.

(5) Which do you like (better, best) coffee or milk?

2 다음 ( ) 안의 형용사를 알맞은 형으로 고쳐 쓰시오.

(1) Tom is the (diligent) boy in his class. _____

(2) Mary is (pretty) than Jane. _____

(3) The (many) we have, the more we want. _____

(4) She is (little) old than my sister. _____

(5) He speaks English (well) than I. _____

3 다음 숫자를 읽으시오.

(1) 222, 222, 222 = _____

(2) 2시 10분 = ① _____ ② _____

(3) 2시 30분 = ① _____ ② _____

(4) 9월 16일 = ① _____ ② _____

(5) 77 = _____

(6) 107 = _____

(7) 2000년 = _____

4 다음에서 잘못된 곳을 바르게 고치시오.

1. big - biger - bigest _____

2. pretty - more pretty - most pretty _____

3. useful - usefuler - usefulest _____

4. bad - less - least _____

Part 6

부사

ADVERB

Chapter 01

부사의 종류

1. You can learn Korean **easily**.	너는 한국어를 쉽게 배울 수 있다.
2. **Where** do you learn English?	당신은 어디에서 영어를 배웁니까?
3. This is the city **where** I was born.	이곳은 내가 태어난 도시이다.

부사는 동사, 형용사, 부사를 수식하는 말로 단순부사, 의문부사, 관계부사 등 3가지가 있다.

1 단순부사 동사, 형용사, 부사 등 다른 말을 수식한다.

① 시간: now, today, tomorrow, ago 등
② 장소: here, there, far, near 등
③ 정도: very, well, much, little 등
④ 양태: easily, quickly, slowly 등
⑤ 횟수: once, often, sometimes 등
⑥ 확언: yes, no, not, never 등

2 의문부사 의문의 뜻을 나타내는 말이다.

① 시간: when
② 장소: where
③ 이유: why
④ 방법: how

3 관계부사 '접속사와 부사'의 역할을 하는 부사로 형용사절을 이끈다.

① 시간: the time when
② 장소: the place where
③ 이유: the reason why
④ 방법: the way that

부사와 형용사의 비교

· You must be **careful** not to make a mistake.	[형용사]
· You must walk **carefully** at night.	[부사]
· This book is **easy**.	[형용사]
· This book is read **easily**.	[부사]

Chapter 02

부사의 형태

1 〈형용사 + ly〉의 형식

1 형용사 뒤에 ly를 그대로 붙인다.

· kind − kindly, slow − slowly, quick − quickly

2 〈자음 + y〉일 때 y를 i로 고쳐 ly를 붙인다.

· easy − easily, happy − happily, merry − merrily

3 '-l'로 끝날 때 ly를 붙인다.

· usual − usually, real − really

4 '-ll'로 끝나면 y만을 붙인다.

· full − fully

5 '-le, -ue'로 끝나면 e를 빼고 ly를 붙인다.

· noble − nobly, true − truly, gentle − gently

6 명사에 ly를 붙여서 부사가 아닌 형용사로 쓰이는 형용사가 많다.

· man − manly, love − lovely, friend − friendly

7 형용사와 부사 두 가지로 쓰이는 것

· day − daily(매일의, 매일), month − monthly(매달의, 매달), kind − kindly(친절한, 친절히)

2 형용사와 같은 형태의 부사

· He is **late** this evening. (형용사: 늦은) / He comes home **late**. (부사: 늦게)
· He is a **fast** runner. (형용사: 빠른) / He runs **fast**. (부사: 빨리)

hard ┌ 어려운, 딱딱한 (형)	well ┌ 건강한 (형)	much ┌ 많은 (형)
└ 열심히 (부)	└ 잘 (부)	└ 많이 (부)
long ┌ 긴 (형)	early ┌ 이른 (형)	enough ┌ 충분한 (형)
└ 오래 (부)	└ 일찍 (부)	└ 충분히 (부)

3 부사의 중복형

· late: 늦은 (형)   late: 늦게 (부)   lately: 최근에 (부)
· hard: 어려운 (형)   hard: 열심히 (부)   hardly: 거의 ~않다 (부)
· high: 높은 (형)   high: 높게 (부)   highly: 대단히 (부)

Pattern Practice

1. Can you tell me the way **kindly**?

2. **When** does she leave Seoul?

3. Do you know **when** she will leave Seoul?

4. I know the day **when** she will leave Seoul.

5. I stood up **when** he came in the room.

6. This is **when** I began to learn English.

7. **Where** are you going?

8. Do you know **where** he is going?

9. **Where** do you think he is going?

10. I know the village **where** he lives.

11. This is **where** he was born.

12. Would you tell me the reason **why** she was late that morning?

13. **Why** are you late this morning?

14. Please tell me **the way** you drive a car.

15. This book is very **hard**.

16. He studies English very **hard**.

17. He **hardly** studies English at home.

18. There is a very **high** mountain.

19. Please jump up as **high** as possible.

20. My father returned home from America **lately**.

1. 다음 영문을 우리말로 옮기시오.

(1) I was late for school yesterday. _____

(2) The subway is ten minutes late. _____

(3) We went on a picnic in late autumn. _____

(4) The late President Lincoln was the greatest man in American history.

_____

(5) She went to bed late yesterday. _____

(6) Don't go out too late at night. _____

(7) Are you interested in English lately? _____

(8) I think English hard. _____

(9) I want to have hard ice cream. _____

(10) You must always study hard in youth. _____

(11) I can hardly understand what he said. _____

(12) He always speaks in a high tone. _____

(13) A jet airplane is flying high in the sky. _____

(14) I have not seen you for a long time. _____

(15) My grandfather lives very long. _____

2. 다음 문장을 영작하시오.

(1) 나는 너에게 영어를 쉽게 가르칠 수 있다. _____

(2) 아침에 일찍 일어나라. _____

(3) 그는 집에서 영어를 매우 열심히 공부한다. _____

(4) 너는 오늘 아침에 왜 늦었니? _____

(5) 나는 어제 아팠어. _____

연습문제

3. 다음 ( ) 안에 각 단어의 부사형을 쓰시오.

(1) kind   (   )
(2) easy   (   )
(3) usual   (   )
(4) full   (   )
(5) true   (   )
(6) slow   (   )
(7) late   (   )
(8) happy   (   )
(9) day   (   )
(10) fast   (   )

(11) beautiful (   )
(12) early   (   )
(13) month   (   )
(14) much   (   )
(15) enough   (   )
(16) careful   (   )
(17) gentle   (   )
(18) long   (   )
(19) high   (   )
(20) quick   (   )

4. 다음 ( ) 안에서 알맞은 말을 고르시오.

(1) I slept (good, well) last night.

(2) She speaks English (pretty, prettily) well.

(3) He gets up (late, lately) this morning.

(4) She thought English (easy, easily).

(5) She can play tennis (easy, easily)

(6) I can (hard, hardly) believe what he said.

(7) I cannot study English (hard, hardly).

(8) He has been to America (late, lately).

(9) This is a (high, highly) good film in Korea.

(10) This is a very (high, highly) building.

5. 다음 문장의 밑줄 친 부분에 유의하여 우리말로 옮기시오.

(1) <u>When</u> will you leave Seoul?   _____

(2) <u>When</u> do you think he will leave Seoul?   _____

(3) <u>When</u> I was young, I liked to paly baseball. _____

(4) Today is the day <u>when</u> he was born.   _____

(5) <u>When</u> is your birthday?   _____

부사의 용법

P·r·e·v·i·e·w

1. He walks fast. (부사 fast가 동사 walk를 수식) 그는 빨리 걷는다.
2. He is very kind. (부사 very가 형용사 kind를 수식) 그는 매우 친절하다.
3. He walks very fast. (부사 very가 부사 fast를 수식) 그는 매우 빨리 걷는다.

부사는 일반적으로 동사, 형용사, 부사를 수식하지만 명사, 대명사, 문장 전체를 수식할 때도 있다.

1 동사를 수식하는 경우

- He runs **slowly**.
- He reads books **rapidly**.

2 형용사를 수식하는 경우

- He is **very** handsome.
- He is a **very** good friend.

3 다른 부사를 수식하는 경우

- She studies **very** hard.
- She swims **very** well.

4 명사를 수식하는 경우

- **Even** a child can do it.
- You must read good books **only**.

5 대명사를 수식하는 경우

- **Only** he can do it.
- Do you want anything **else**?

6 문장 전체를 수식하는 경우

- **Happily** he did not die.
  cf. He did not die happily.

Part 6 부사 Adverb

Chapter 04 부사의 위치

P·r·e·v·i·e·w

1. He is **very** strong.	그는 매우 강하다.
2. He must study **hard**.	그는 열심히 공부해야 한다.
3. You had better **take off** your hat in the room.	방안에서는 모자를 벗는 것이 좋다.
4. She is **always** busy these days.	그녀는 요즘 항상 바쁘다.
5. I go **to school by bus at seven in the morning**.	나는 오늘 아침 7시에 학교에 버스로 간다.

1 형용사, 부사를 수식할 때는 그 앞에 온다.

· He is a **very** strong man.
· She studies English **very** hard.

2 자동사를 수식하는 부사는 그 뒤에 오고, 타동사를 수식하는 부사는 목적어 뒤에 온다.

· She walks **fast**.
· She is walking very **fast** in the morning.
· He wrote a letter **quickly**.
· He read the book **easily**.

3 〈타동사 + 부사〉가 동사구(2어 동사)로 결합될 때 목적어가 명사이면 부사 앞뒤에 올 수 있으나,
목적어가 대명사이면 부사 앞에만 놓아야 한다.

· **Take off** your hat. (○)
  Take your hat **off**. (○)

· **Put on** your overcoats. (○)
  Put your overcoats **on**. (○)

· **Take off** it. (×)
  Take it **off**. (○)

· **Put on** it. (×)
  Put it **on**. (○)

pick up (~을 줍다)	put in (~을 넣다)	take out (~을 꺼내다)
turn on (~을 켜다)	put off (연기하다)	turn off (~을 끄다)

4 빈도부사와 정도부사는 be동사(조동사) 뒤에 오고, have동사(일반동사) 앞에 온다.

□ 빈도부사: always, often, usually, sometimes, seldom, never 등

□ 정도부사: quite, almost, hardly, scarcely 등

① 빈도부사와 정도부사는 be동사나 조동사 뒤에 온다.
  · He is **always** late for school.
  · She will **never** go to the mountain by herself.

② 빈도부사와 정도부사는 have동사나 일반동사 앞에 온다.
  · He **always** goes to school by bus.
  · She **usually** has much money.
     cf. She has **often** bought some flowers.

5 일정한 시간을 나타내는 부사는 문장 맨 앞이나 문장 뒤에 놓는다.

  · **Yesterday** I went to school by bus.
  · I went to school by bus **yesterday**.

6 부사가 두 개 이상 겹칠 때에는 〈장소 + 방법 + 시간〉의 어순으로 하고, 시간부사가 여러 개 올 때는 〈시간(작은 단위) + 시간(큰 단위)〉의 어순으로 한다.

  · I came **home by car at five in the evening**.
  · He arrived **here safely late last night**.

7 구와 절을 수식할 때는 부사가 앞에 온다.

  · She began her homework **soon** after dinner.
  · I don't like her **simply** because she is not honest.

8 문장 전체를 수식할 때는 부사를 문장 맨 앞에 놓기도 하고, 동사 앞에 놓기도 한다.

  · **Fortunately** he did not die.
  · He **fortunately** did not die.

perhaps (아마도)	really (정말, 실제로)	possibly (아마도)
certainly (틀림없이)	fortunately (다행히도)	unfortunately (불행히도)

9 enough는 항상 형용사와 부사 뒤에 위치한다.

  · She plays tennis well **enough**.
  · He is kind **enough** to tell me the way.

Pattern Practice

1. **Even** a lady can make such a thing.

2. What **else** do you want to do?

3. **Only** he can solve the problem.

4. He **only** loves me.

5. He loves **only** me.

6. She swims **very** slowly.

7. She speaks English **very** slowly.

8. Please **pick up** the pencil.

9. Please **turn** the light **off**.

10. Please **pick** it **up**.

11. He is **always** asleep in the class.

12. She **always** plays the piano after school.

13. He has **never** been in London.

14. **Happily** he did not die.

15. He did not die **happily**.

16. There **once** lived an old man in a small village.

17. She goes **to school by subway at six every morning**.

18. He has **enough** money to buy a car.

19. He is rich **enough** to buy a car.

20. She studied **enough**, but she failed in the examination.

1. 다음 영문을 우리말로 옮기시오.

   (1) Even a child can do it. _____

   (2) Do you want anything else? _____

   (3) She walks slowly in the park. _____

   (4) She speaks English very slowly. _____

   (5) Happily he did not die. _____

   (6) He did not die happily. _____

   (7) He goes to school by subway every morning. _____

   (8) There once lived a king named Arthur in England. _____

   (9) He is usually late for school. _____

   (10) He usually plays baseball after school. _____

   (11) Please turn off the radio while I am studying. _____

   (12) Please pick it up. _____

   (13) Yesterday I went home at seven in the evening. _____

   (14) I went to church at 9:30 yesterday. _____

   (15) She always goes to the supermarket at five in the afternoon.

   _____

2. 다음 문장을 영작하시오.

   (1) 그녀는 매우 빨리 걷는다. _____

   (2) 그녀는 영어를 매우 천천히 말한다. _____

   (3) 나는 매일 아침 걸어서 학교에 간다. _____

   (4) 그는 항상 책을 읽는다. _____

   (5) 그는 항상 바쁘다. _____

05 주의할 부사의 용법 I

P·r·e·v·i·e·w

1. **There** is a book on the desk.	책상 위에 책이 있다.
2. **Here** is a book.	여기에 책이 있다.
3. This book is **very** interesting.	이 책은 매우 재미있다.
4. I am **much** interested in this book.	나는 이 책에 대단히 흥미가 있다.

1 장소의 부사 there, here

· **There** is a car.　　　　　　**There** are cars.

· **Here** is a car.　　　　　　**Here** are cars.

· **There** is a car **there**.　　　**There** are cars **there**.

· **There** is a car **here**.　　　**There** are cars **here**.

· **There** lived a man in this village.

2 정도의 부사 very, much

1 very의 용법

① 형용사와 부사를 수식

② 형용사와 부사의 원급을 수식

③ 현재분사를 수식

· He is **very** good.　　　　· He runs **very** fast.

· She is **very** tall.　　　　· The music is **very** interesting.

2 much의 용법

① 동사를 수식

② 형용사와 부사의 비교급, 최상급을 수식

③ 과거분사를 수식

· I like him very **much**.　　· He runs **much** faster than I.

· She is **much** the tallest of all.　· She is **much** interested in the music.

TIP

I am very tired.

① 형용사화한 과거분사 tired, pleased, worried, delighted 등은 비록 과거분사의 형태이지만 very로 수식한다.

② afraid, preferable 등은 much로 수식한다.

Chapter 06 주의할 부사의 용법 2

P · r · e · v · i · e · w

1. I saw him two weeks **ago**.	나는 그를 2주 전에 보았다.
2. I had seen him **before**.	나는 그를 전에 보았던 적이 있었다.
3. I have **already** done my homework.	나는 벌써 숙제를 끝마쳤다.
4. I have not finished the work **yet**.	나는 그 일을 아직 끝마치지 못했다.

1 ago, before, since의 용법

1 ago 　지금부터 '~전'이란 뜻이고, 과거 시제에 쓰인다.
2 before 　과거의 어느 시점부터 '그전'이란 뜻이고, 과거완료 시제에 쓰인다.
3 since 　현재완료 시제에 쓰인다.

· She died five years **ago**.
· She said that she had seen a tiger **before**.
· He has lived in Seoul **since** last year.

▶▶ ago는 언제나 명사(숫자)와 함께 쓰인다. before는 단독으로 쓰이면 막연히 '전에'란 뜻이다.

2 already, yet, still의 용법

1 already 　완료형에서 긍정문에는 '벌써, 이미 ~했다'로 쓰이고, 의문문에서는 '벌써'로 해석하며 놀람과 의외를 나타낸다.
2 yet 　완료형에서 부정문에는 '아직 ~않았다'로 쓰이고, 의문문에서는 '벌써 ~했느냐'로 쓰인다.
3 still 　긍정문에서 '아직'으로 쓰인다.

· He has **already** finished the work.　(긍정문)
· Has he finished the work **already**?　(놀라움)
· Have you finished the work **yet**?　(의문문)
· I have not written the book **yet**.　(부정문)
· I am **still** reading the book.　(긍정문)

▶▶ 물론 already, yet 등이 일반 시제에서도 쓰인다.

Part 6 부사 Adverb

Pattern Practice

1. **There** is a white house on the hill.

2. **Here** is a white house.

3. There are white houses **there**.

4. There are white houses **here**.

5. She is a **very** good tennis player.

6. Thank you **very** much for your kindness.

7. He could skate **very** fast on the lake.

8. This is a **very** interesting novel.

9. She was **much** surprised to hear the news.

10. He is **very** pleased to have a good friend.

11. She was **much** afraid of the dog.

12. He died seven years **ago**.

13. It is seven years **since** he died.

14. He has been dead **for** seven years.

15. Seven years have passed **since** he died.

16. Have you read the book through **already**?

17. Have you written the book **yet**?

18. I have **already** read through the book.

19. I have not built the building **yet**.

20. He is **still** writing a letter.

연습문제

1. 다음 영문을 우리말로 옮기시오.

   (1) There is a book on the desk. _____

   (2) There are many books. _____

   (3) There are many books there. _____

   (4) There is much milk here. _____

   (5) Here is much milk. _____

   (6) This is a very exciting game. _____

   (7) People in the stadium are much excited. _____

   (8) She is very pleased to see her son again. _____

   (9) She is much afraid of a dog. _____

   (10) Have you done your homework already? _____

   (11) Have you finished the work yet? _____

   (12) He has already built the building. _____

   (13) I have not done my homework yet. _____

   (14) I met him in London two years ago. _____

   (15) She has been ill since last month. _____

2. 다음 문장을 영작하시오.

   (1) 나는 2주 전에 그를 만났다. _____

   (2) 여기에 많은 오렌지들이 있습니다. _____

   (3) 그녀는 음악에 많은 흥미를 가지고 있다. _____

   (4) 이 책은 매우 재미있다. _____

   (5) 나는 아직 숙제를 마치지 못했다. _____

3. 다음 ( ) 안에서 알맞은 말을 고르시오.

(1) This book is (very, much) interesting.

(2) I am (very, much) interested in this book.

(3) She is (very, much) tired today.

(4) He is (very, much) taller than I.

(5) He runs (very, much) fast.

(6) He is (very, much) pleased to have many books.

(7) She is (very, much) afraid of a dog.

(8) I met her three weeks (ago, before).

(9) They have lived in Seoul (since, before) last year.

(10) I have (already, yet) finished the work.

(11) He has not finished the work (already, yet).

(12) He said that he had bought the skate (ago, before).

(13) He is (very, much) the tallest of all.

(14) Are you tired? (Yes, No), I'm not.

(15) Aren't you tired? (Yes, No), I'm not.

4. 다음 ( ) 안에 문장이 맞으면 ○, 틀리면 ×를 써 넣으시오.

(1) Please take off your hat.　　　　(　)

(2) Please take off it.　　　　(　)

(3) Please take your hat off.　　　　(　)

(4) Please take it off.　　　　(　)

(5) I met him two days before.　　　　(　)

(6) She went to school a week ago.　　　　(　)

(7) Tom swims very faster than Jack.　　　　(　)

(8) Tom is much older than Jack.　　　　(　)

(9) Jane has not seen the tiger already.　　　　(　)

(10) Has Jane seen the tiger already?　　　　(　)

주의할 부사의 용법 3

Part 6 부사 Adverb

P · r · e · v · i · e · w

1. I am reading a book, **too**.	나도 역시 책을 읽고 있습니다.
2. She likes oranges. **So** do I.	그녀는 오렌지를 좋아한다. 나 역시 그렇다.
	(= 나 역시 오렌지를 좋아한다.)
3. I can **scarcely** see the house.	나는 그 집을 거의 볼 수 없다.
4. I go **home** at five this evening.	나는 오늘 저녁 5시에 집에 간다.

1 too, either의 용법

1 too   역시, 또한 (긍정문, 의문문) / 너무 ~하게 (긍정문, 의문문, 부정문)
2 either   역시, 또한 (부정문)
3 also   역시, 또한 (긍정문, 의문문, 부정문)

- She is a doctor, **too**.
- She is not a doctor, **either**.
- Is she a doctor, **too**?
- It is **too** cold this winter.

- She is **also** a doctor.
- She is not **also** a doctor.
- Is she **also** a doctor?
- It was not **too** cold last winter.

2 so, neither의 용법

1 so   역시 ~하다   (긍정문)
2 neither   역시 ~하지 않다 (부정문)

- He is happy.
- He is not happy.
- He likes her.
- He doesn't like her.

- **So** am I. (= I am happy, too.)
- **Neither** am I. (= I am not happy, either.)
- **So** do. I. (= I like her, too.)
- **Neither** do I. (= I don't like her, either.)

3 scarcely(= hardly), seldom(= rarely)의 용법

- I can **scarcely** swim across the river.
- He **rarely** comes to my house.

4 so, too의 용법

〈so + 형(부) + that ~〉 대단히 ~해서 ~하다

- He is **so** fast **that** he can catch his dog.
- He is **so** poor **that** he **cannot** go to college. = He is **too** poor **to** go to college.

Pattern Practice

1. The work is **already** finished.

2. Is it twelve o'clock **already**?

3. He plays the violin, **too**.

4. I don't play the violin, **either**.

5. She is **also** a good pianist.

6. She **also** plays the piano well.

7. I can **hardly** walk to school by myself.

8. She is **seldom** late for school.

9. He **seldom** looks happy.

10. He takes a walk very **seldom** lately.

11. This hat is **too** big for me.

12. This book is **too** difficult for him **to** read.

13. This book is **so** difficult **that** he **cannot** read it.

14. He is **too** old **to** go out by himself at night.

15. He is **so** old **that** he **cannot** go out by himself at night.

16. He runs **too** fast for me **to** catch him.

17. He runs **so** fast **that** I **cannot** catch him.

18. He goes to church with his mother **on** Sunday.

19. She is kind. **So am I**.

20. She doesn't read books. **Neither do I**.

연습문제

1. 다음 영문을 우리말로 옮기시오.

(1) He plays the violin, too. _____

(2) He plays tennis well. So do I. _____

(3) She is reading a book, too. _____

(4) She is reading a book. So am I. _____

(5) She can not play the piano, either. _____

(6) She can not play tennis well. Neither can I. _____

(7) He doesn't play baseball. Neither do I. _____

(8) I am seldom late for school. _____

(9) She is too old to go out for a walk. _____

(10) This book is too difficult for him to read. _____

(11) This book is so difficult that he cannot read it. _____

(12) She can hardly walk to school by herself. _____

(13) The house is already built. _____

(14) He thought the game exciting. _____

(15) I believed that he was an honest man. _____

2. 다음 문장을 영작하시오.

(1) 그의 어머니도 역시 요리를 잘 한다. _____

(2) 나도 역시 피아노를 칠 수 없다. _____

(3) 나는 매주 어머니와 교회에 간다. _____

(4) 그는 너무 나이가 들어서 일할 수 없다. _____

(5) 그는 좀처럼 책을 읽지 않는다. _____

3. 다음 두 문장의 내용이 같아지도록 ( ) 안에 알맞은 말을 써 넣으시오.

(1) She is diligent.

I am, too. = (　　　) am I.

(2) She is not tall.

I am not, either. = (　　　) am I.

(3) He likes books.

I do, too. = (　　　) do I.

(4) He doesn't like books.

I don't, either. = (　　　) do I.

(5) He is too weak to swim in the pool.

He is (　　) weak (　　) he (　　) (　　) swim in the pool.

(6) This book is too difficult for him to read.

This book is (　　) difficult (　　) (　　) cannot read (　　).

(7) He can hardly read this book.

He can (　　) read this book.

(8) I believe him honest.

I believe (　　) (　　) is honest.

(9) She is kind enough to tell me the story.

She is (　　) kind that she tells me the story.

(10) She is seldom late for school.

She is (　　) late for school.

4. 다음 우리말을 참고하여 ( ) 안에 알맞은 말을 써 넣으시오.

(1) This English book is (　　) hard (　　) read.
이 영어 책은 너무 어려워서 읽을 수 없다.

(2) He is (　　) lazy (　　) he cannot succeed.
그는 너무 게을러서 성공할 수 없다.

(3) He can play tennis well. (　　) can I.
그는 테니스를 잘 칠 수 있다. 나도 그렇다.

(4) He plays baseball well. (　　) do I.
그는 야구를 잘 한다. 나도 그렇다.

(5) He doesn't play baseball. (　　) do I.
그는 야구를 하지 않는다. 나도 그렇다.

1. 다음 영문을 우리말로 옮기시오.

(1) Do you know the city where he lives now? _____

(2) My grandmother is still alive. _____

(3) My friend has come from Japan lately. _____

(4) I can hardly see Jane after graduation. _____

(5) This book is too difficult to read. _____

2. 다음 문장을 영작하시오.

(1) 당신은 언제 서울을 떠날 예정입니까? _____

(2) 나는 5월에 서울을 떠날 예정입니다. _____

(3) 너는 왜 매일 학교에 늦니? _____

(4) 그는 너무 가난해서 대학교에 갈 수 없다. _____

(5) 나는 학교에서 열심히 공부했다. _____

3. 다음 ( ) 안에서 알맞은 것을 고르시오.

(1) She played the piano (good, well) last night.

(2) She thought English (easy, easily).

(3) The game was (very, much) exciting.

(4) The house has not been built (already, yet).

(5) I met him two days (ago, before) downtown.

4. 다음 문장에서 잘못된 곳이 있으면 바르게 고치시오.

(1) Please pick up pencils. _____

(2) Please pick up them. _____

(3) He has been to New York late. _____

(4) She learned English easy. _____

(5) This blouse looks well. _____

Part 6 부사 Adverb

Part 7

전치사

PREPOSITION

01 전치사의 기능

P·r·e·v·i·e·w

1. I go **to school with her**.	나는 그녀와 함께 학교에 간다.
2. I am proud **of being** a teacher.	나는 선생님인 것을 자랑으로 여긴다.

전치사는 명사, 대명사, 명사 상당어구의 앞에 놓여서 그 전후에 있는 말의 관계를 나타낸다.

1 전치사의 역할

1 형용사구와 부사구로 쓰인다.

2 전치사의 목적어로 명사, 대명사, 동명사, 부정사, 명사구, 명사절 등이 온다.

2 전치사의 위치

1 목적어 앞에 올 경우 전치사는 원칙적으로 목적어 앞에 온다.

2 목적어 뒤에 올 경우 전치사는 그 목적어 앞에 두는 것이 원칙이지만 그 뒤에 오는 경우가 있다. 의문사와 관계대명사가 목적어일 때, 부정사가 형용사구를 이룰 때, 동사구가 수동태를 이룰 때이다.

3 전치사의 종류 (형태상의 분류)

1 단순전치사 at, in, to, on, with, for, up 등

2 이중전치사 from behind, from under, till after 등

3 구전치사 because of, in front of, out of, in the middle of 등

4 전치사의 종류 (의미상의 분류)

1 시간을 나타내는 전치사
- at, in, on, from, since, after, till, by, for, during, through, within, about, round 등

2 장소를 나타내는 전치사
- at, in, on, beneath, over, under, above, below, up, down, into, out of, across, through, along, between, among 등

3 그 밖의 전치사 원인(이유), 목적, 결과, 재료(원료), 수단(방법), 단위, 출신(출처) 등

Chapter 02 전치사의 역할

P·r·e·v·i·e·w

1. The house **on the hill** is very beautiful.	언덕 위에 있는 그 집은 매우 아름답다.
2. There is a house **on the hill**.	언덕 위에 집이 있다.
3. I go **to school** by bus every day.	나는 매일 버스로 학교에 간다.
4. I went to the supermarket **with her**.	나는 그녀와 함께 슈퍼마켓에 갔다.
5. He went away **without saying good-bye**.	그는 작별 인사 없이 가버렸다.
6. I was **about to leave**.	나는 막 떠나려 했다.
7. **After school**, we played baseball.	방과 후, 우리는 야구를 했다.

1 형용사구와 부사구   형용사구는 보통 앞의 명사를 수식하고 부사구는 동사, 형용사, 부사 및 문장을 수식한다.

· The book **on the desk** is mine.
· The book is **of use** to me.
· The book is **on the desk**.
· London is famous **for its fog**.
· He swims well **for a beginner**.
· **To my surprise**, they won the game.

2 전치사의 목적어   전치사 뒤에 명사, 대명사, 동명사 등이 와서 전치사의 목적어를 만든다. 이외에도 부정사, 명사구, 명사절, 부사 등이 온다.

▶▶ 주의할 점: 전치사 다음에 명사, 대명사는 반드시 목적격이 와야 한다.

· I live **in the house**.
· I played tennis **with her**.
· I am fond **of playing baseball**.
· I had no choice **but to marry him**. (부정사)
· He looked at me **from above his glasses**. (명사구)
· Success depends **on how you do your work well**. (명사절)
· How far is it **from here** to your house? (부사)

Part 7 전치사 Preposition

165

3 전치사의 품사 전환

1 전치사가 부사로   목적어가 없는 전치사는 부사로 취급한다.

- He is **in** the room. (전치사)
- Please come **in**. (부사)
- Let's go **along the street**. (전치사)
- Let's go **along**. (부사)

2 부사로 전용된 부사와 대명사의 관계   〈타동사 + 부사〉 형식의 2어동사이다.

① 목적어가 명사일 때: 부사는 명사 앞뒤 어느 쪽이나 좋다.
② 목적어가 대명사일 때: 부사는 반드시 목적어 뒤에 온다.

- Pick **up the pencil**. (○)/ Pick **the pencil up**. (○)
- Pick **up it**. (×) / Pick **it up**. (○)
- Take **off your hat**. (○) / Take **your hat off**. (○)
- Take **off it**. (×) / Take **it off**. (○)

      cf. She **went up** the hill. (○)
         She **went** the hill **up**. (×)
         She **went up it**. (○)
         She **went it up**. (×)

         ▶▶ up은 전치사이므로 〈동사 + 전치사〉 = 타동사구이다.

3 전치사가 부사, 접속사의 구실을 하는 것   after, before, since 등

- He arrived **after me**. (전치사)
- He arrived **after**. (부사)
- He arrived **after** she had left here. (접속사)

- I brush my teeth **before** breakfast. (전치사)
- I brush my teeth **before** I have breakfast. (접속사)
- I have seen her **before**. (부사)

- I have been happy **since** my marriage. (전치사)
- I have been happy ever **since**. (부사)
- I have been happy **since** I married her. (접속사)

전치사의 위치

1. She is listening **to** music.	그녀는 음악을 듣고 있다.
2. **What** are you looking **for**?	당신은 무엇을 찾고 있습니까?
3. This is the house **which** he lives **in**.	이것은 그가 살고 있는 집이다.
4. I have no friend to play **with**.	나는 같이 놀 친구가 없다.
5. The dog was run **over** by a truck.	그 개는 트럭에 치였다.

전치사는 원칙적으로 그 목적어 앞에 놓이지만 목적어 뒤에 놓일 때가 있다.

1 목적어 앞에 두는 경우   전치사는 원칙적으로 목적어 앞에 둔다.

· I went shopping **with** my mother.
· He has lived **in** Seoul for ten years.

2 목적어 뒤에 두는 경우   의문사와 관계대명사가 목적어일 때, 부정사가 형용사구를 이룰 때, 동사구가 수동태로 될 때 목적어 뒤에 둔다.

· Whom are you looking **at**?
· Do you know the man whom she is fond **of**?
· I have no house to live **in**.
· He was laughed **at** by her.

TIP

전치사의 강세
❶ 대명사 앞에 온 전치사에 강세가 온다.
   · Please look **at me**.
      cf. Please look **at the map**.
❷ 〈동사 + 부사〉의 2어동사일 때 부사에 강세를 둔다.
   · Please come **in**.
   · Please pick it **up**.
❸ 대조적으로 쓰인 전치사에는 강세가 온다.
   · Is there a book **on** the table or **under** the table?

전치사의 종류 (형태상의 분류)

1. I get up early **in** the morning.	나는 아침 일찍 일어난다.
2. The cat ran out **from under** the table.	고양이가 탁자 밑에서 뛰어 나왔다.
3. I met him **in front of** that building.	나는 저 건물 앞에서 그를 만났다.

1 단순전치사   at, in, to, on, for, with, up 등

- I go **to** school **at** seven **in** the morning.
- I have curry and rice **for** lunch.
- He went **up** the mountain **with** his friends.

2 이중전치사   from behind, from under, till after 등

- She came out **from behind** the curtain.
- The mouse came out **from under** the desk.
- I will wait for you **till after** seven.

3 구전치사   because of, in front of, out of, in the middle of 등

- **Because of** rain, I can not wait for her **in front of** the office.
- He looked **out of** the window.
- The light is **in the middle of** the living room.

> **TIP** 중요한 이중전치사와 구전치사
> ❶ 이중전치사
> - since before the war (전쟁 전부터)
> - for over ten years (10년 이상에 걸쳐)
> - from among them (그들 가운데로부터)
> - from before Sunday (일요일 이전부터)
> - from beyond the river (강 저쪽으로부터)
>
> ❷ 구전치사
> - in spite of (~에도 불구하고)
> - instead of (~의 대신에)
> - owing to (~ 때문에)
> - on account of (~ 때문에)
> - according to (~에 의하면)
> - by way of (~을 경유하여)

1. My father **in** the living room is reading a newspaper.

2. My mother is watching TV **in** the living room.

3. My sister wants to go **to** the department store **with** him.

4. He is proud **of** writing a book.

5. She is listening to music **in** her room.

6. Please come **in**.

7. Put it **on**, please.

8. You must wash your face and hands **before** you go to bed.

9. You wash your face and hands **before** bed time.

10. I have slept without washing my face and hands **before**.

11. Do you know the house **in** which he lives?

12. Do you know the house which he lives **in**?

13. Do you know the house for him to live **in**?

14. My mother always goes shopping **in** the afternoon.

15. I would wait for the bus **till after** seven thirty in the morning.

16. Mr. Bang has been teaching English **for over twenty years**.

17. She studied hard **in spite of** being ill.

18. I went to New York **by way of** Hawaii.

19. **Because of** the rain, I could not go to the party.

연습문제

1. 다음 영문을 우리말로 옮기시오.

(1) She has gone to Italy to study music. _____

(2) The car in the shop was made in Korea. _____

(3) There are a lot of Korean products in the department store.

_____

(4) She is afraid of speaking English at the party. _____

(5) Please turn off the radio while I am studying. _____

(6) He has been happy since his marriage. _____

(7) He has been happy ever since. _____

(8) He has been happy since he married her. _____

(9) Who is she looking for? _____

(10) I have many friends to play baseball with. _____

(11) The ship appeared from behind the big rock. _____

(12) There is a policeman in the middle of the street. _____

(13) I began to learn Chinese from before Sunday. _____

(14) According to today's paper, there was a big fire in Busan.

_____

(15) He succeeded owing to his father's help. _____

2. 다음 문장을 영작하시오.

(1) 비 때문에, 우리는 소풍을 갈 수 없다. _____

(2) 나의 여동생은 방에서 그녀의 친구들과 같이 놀고 있다. _____

(3) 나는 저녁 식사 후에 텔레비전을 본다. _____

(4) 나는 살 집이 없다. _____

(5) 연필 좀 집어 주세요. _____

전치사의 종류 (의미상의 분류)

Chapter 05

P·r·e·v·i·e·w

1. I want to have a party **on** my birthday. (시간)	나는 내 생일에 파티를 열길 원한다.
2. I live at Sillim-dong **in** Seoul. (장소)	나는 서울 신림동에서 산다.
3. She has been ill in bed **with** cold. (원인)	그녀는 감기 때문에 앓고 있다.
4. He goes out **for** a walk. (목적)	그는 산책하러 나간다.
5. He overworked himself **to** death. (결과)	그는 과로해서 죽었다.
6. The desk is made **of** wood. (재료)	그 책상은 나무로 만들어져 있다.
7. He goes to school **by** bus. (수단)	그는 버스로 학교에 간다.
8. Sugar is sold **by** the pound. (단위)	설탕은 파운드로 팔린다.
9. She came **from** Paris. (출신)	그녀는 파리 출신이다.

1 때, 시간을 나타내는 전치사

1 at, in, on

① at: 시, 분, 정오 등의 비교적 짧은 시간을 나타낸다.

· I get up **at** six every morning.

at seven (7시에)	at sunset (해질 무렵에)
at noon (정오에)	at midnight (자정에)
at dawn (새벽에)	at present (현재에)
at night (밤에)	at Christmas (성탄절에)

② in: 월, 년, 계절, 오전, 오후 등의 비교적 긴 시간을 나타낸다.

· I would like to swim **in** summer.

in September (9월에)	in the morning (오전에)
in spring (봄에)	in my life (내 생애에)
in 2019 (2019년에)	in the 21st century (21세기에)

③ on: 요일, 날짜, 특정한 오전과 오후 등 일정한 일시를 나타낸다.

· I go to church **on** Sunday.

on the 16th of September (9월 16일에)
on Saturday evening (토요일 저녁에)
on New Year' Day (설날에)

2 till(until), by

① till(~까지): 동작과 상태의 계속을 나타낸다.

　　· I will wait here **till** nine.

② by(~까지는): 동작의 완료를 나타낸다.

　　· I will come back **by** nine.

3 for, during, through

① for(~ 동안): 일정한 기간을 나타낸다. 보통 〈for + 수사(a) + 시간 명사〉

　　· I have lived in Seoul **for** ten years.

② during(~ 동안): 어떤 상태가 계속되는 특정한 기간을 나타낸다. 보통 〈during + 특정한 기간의 단수명사〉

　　· I will stay here **during** the summer vacation.

③ through(~ 동안 죽): '처음부터 끝까지 내내'란 뜻을 나타낸다.

　　· It kept raining **through** the night.

4 from, since

① from(~로부터): 일이 시작되는 기점을 나타낸다.

　　· I lived in Seoul **from** 2009 **to** 2019.

　　· He worked **from** morning **till** night.

　　cf. School begins **at** eight.

　　　　Let's begin **with** page 38.

② since(~부터 죽): 과거부터 현재까지 계속을 나타낸다. 보통 완료형과 더불어 쓰인다.

　　· She has been ill in bed **since** last week.

5 in, within

① in(~이 지나면, 지나서): 시간의 경과를 나타낸다.

　　· He will be back **in** a month.

② within(~의 기간 이내에): 일정한 기간 이내를 나타낸다.

　　· He will be back **within** a month.

2 장소를 나타내는 전치사

1 at, in

① at: 비교적 좁은 장소를 나타낸다.
- He arrived **at** Incheon International Airport.

② in: 비교적 넓은 장소를 나타낸다.
- She arrived **in** New York.

2 on, beneath, over, under, above, below, up, down

① on: 접촉해 있는 위에
- The telephone is **on** the table.

② beneath: 접촉해 있는 아래에
- I put the pillow **beneath** my head.

③ over: 바로 위에
- The bridge is **over** the river.

④ under: 바로 아래에
- The boat is **under** the bridge.

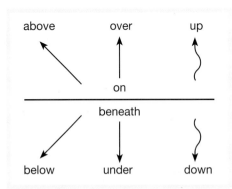

⑤ above: 보다 위쪽에
- The sun has risen **above** the hill.

⑥ below: 보다 아래쪽에
- The sun is sinking **below** the hill.

⑦ up: 위쪽으로 (운동을 수반)
- Please stand **up** quickly.

⑧ down: 아래쪽으로 (운동을 수반)
- Please sit **down** quickly.

3 in, into, out of

① in(~안에, ~안에서): 속에 있는 상태를 나타낸다.
- He is **in** the room.

② into(~의 안으로): 속으로 들어가는 동작을 나타낸다.
- He came **into** the room.

③ out of(~의 밖으로): 밖으로 나오는 동작을 나타낸다.
- He went **out of** the room.
- Get **out of** here.

4 between, among

① between(~의 사이에): 두 개의 사이를 나타낸다.

· He sat **between** Mary and Jane.

② among(~의 사이에): 셋 이상의 사이를 나타낸다.

· He sat **among** the girls.

5 across, through, along

① across (~을 가로질러)

· He went **across** the street.

② through (~을 통과하여)

· The train passed **through** the tunnel.

③ along (~을 따라)

· I was walking **along** the street.

6 to, for, toward

① to(~에, ~으로): 도착 지점을 나타낸다. (보통 go, come 등의 동사)

· She went **to** Hawaii.

② for(~으로 향하여): 행선지를 나타낸다. (보통 start, leave 등의 동사)

· She started **for** Hawaii.

③ toward(~쪽으로): 운동의 방향을 나타낸다.

· She went **toward** school.

7 round, around, about (round와 around는 엄격한 구별 없이 혼용된다.)

① round(~을 돌아서): 동작을 나타낸다.

· They ran **round** the pond.

② around(~주위에): 정지된 상태를 나타낸다.

· They sat **around** the table.

③ about(~의 주위에, 이리저리): 막연한 주위를 나타낸다.

· They walked **about** the street.

8 before, behind, after

① before: ~앞에(= in front of)

· He sat **before** the table.

② behind: ~뒤에(= at the back of)

· He sat **behind** the door.

③ after: ~의 뒤를 쫓아

· The policeman ran **after** the thief.

Pattern Practice

1. He was born **on** September 16, 2006.

2. He will be back **by** seven in the evening.

3. She has been ill **for** a month.

4. He has been ill **since** last month.

5. I will write the book **within** a month.

6. I live **at** Sillim-dong **in** Seoul, Korea.

7. There are four jet planes **above** us now.

8. The squirrels are running **up** and **down** on the tree.

9. He went **into** the room by himself at night.

10. He swam **across** the river.

11. I have passed **through** a wood.

12. She has gone **to** America.

13. He started **for** L.A. last year.

14. The earth goes **round** the sun.

15. The dog ran **after** the rabbit.

16. I will wait him **till** nine in the evening.

17. I had a good time **during** my summer vacation.

18. My brother studied hard **from** morning **till** night.

19. There is a fly **on** the ceiling.

1. 다음 영문을 우리말로 옮기시오.

(1) I will wait for him till six in the evening. _____

(2) I will be back by six in the evening. _____

(3) I am going to the sea during my summer vacation. _____

(4) It kept raining through the night. _____

(5) She will come back in a year. _____

(6) He is the first Korean to fly across the Pacific. _____

(7) They went through the jungle. _____

(8) While I was walking along the street, I met her. _____

(9) The last train started for Busan. _____

(10) The children sat around the table. _____

(11) The earth goes round the sun. _____

(12) He sat between Jane and Mary. _____

(13) I picked him up among them. _____

(14) They walked about all day long. _____

(15) I sat behind her in the theater. _____

2. 다음 문장을 영작하시오.

(1) 탁자 위에 두 권의 책이 있다. _____

(2) 나는 비행기 한 대가 산 너머로 날아가고 있는 것을 보았다. _____

(3) 그는 나에게 일어나라고 했다. _____

(4) 나는 밤 10시에 집에 왔다. _____

(5) 그는 서울 신림동에서 10년 동안 살아왔다. _____

3 그 밖의 전치사

1 원인, 이유 at, over, from, through, of, for, with

① at(~을 보고, ~을 듣고): 감정적인 원인을 나타낸다.
- I was surprised **at** the news.

② over(~ 때문에, ~에 대하여): 감정의 원인이 되는 사건을 나타낸다.
- She is crying **over** the loss of her son.

③ from(~ 때문에): 질병, 고통 등의 직접적인 원인을 나타낸다.
- He died **from** drinking too much.
- She died **from** overwork.

④ through(~ 때문에): 간접적인 원인을 나타낸다. (부주의, 태만, 과오 등)
- He was dismissed **through** carelessness.

⑤ of(~ 때문에): 어떤 질병이 원인이 되는 경우
- She died **of** cancer.

⑥ for(~ 때문에): 내면적, 심리적 원인을 나타낸다.
- She wept **for** joy.

⑦ with(~ 때문에): 몸에 미치는 외부적 원인을 나타낸다.
- He caught cold **with** cold rain.

2 목적 for, after, on

① for(~을 위하여): 목적, 추구를 나타낸다.
- He sends **for** a doctor.

② after(~을 쫓아): 추구, 추적을 나타낸다.
- He who runs **after** two hares will catch neither.

③ on(~을 하러): 용무, 소풍, 여행 등의 목적에 쓰인다.
- I went to America **on** business.

> on an errand (심부름으로)   on a picnic (소풍으로)   on a tour (여행으로)

3 결과 to, into

① to(~으로 되다): 동작의 결과를 나타낸다.
- He overworked himself **to** death.

② into(~으로 되다): 변화의 결과를 나타낸다.
- Heat changes ice **into** water.

4 방법, 수단, 행위자 by, with, through

① by(~에 의하여, ~으로): 수동태에서는 행위자로, 능동태에서는 수단으로
  • She was killed **by** a robber.
  • She goes to school **by** bus.

② with(~으로): 도구, 신체의 기관과 같이 사용된다.
  • He was killed **with** a knife.
  • We see **with** our eyes, and hear with our ears.

③ through(~을 통하여): 수단과 매개물을 나타낸다.
  • I went to college **through** my uncle's help.
  • I looked out **through** the window.

5 재료, 원료 of, from, into

① of(물리적 변화): be made of ~으로 만들어져 있다
  • The desk is made **of** wood.

② from(화학적 변화): be made from ~으로 만들어져 있다
  • Butter is made **from** milk.

③ into (물리적 변화와 화학적 변화에 관계없이 쓰인다.)
  • Milk is made **into** butter.

6 계량, 단위 by, for

① by(~으로): 〈by + 계량 단위〉의 형태를 취한다.
  • They sell meat **by** the pound.

② for(~에): 교환의 대가로 쓰인다.
  • I bought the radio **for** thirty dollars.
    cf. I bought the radio **at the price of** thirty dollars.
    I paid thirty dollars **for** the radio.

7 출신, 출처 from, of

① from(~의 출신): 〈from + 지명〉의 형태를 취한다.
  • Where are you **from**?
  • I am **from** Seoul.

② of(~의 출신): 〈of + 가문, 혈통〉의 형태를 취한다.
  • He comes **of** a good family.

4 전치사가 있는 숙어

1 〈동사 + 전치사〉의 형태

① agree with + 사람: ~에 동의하다
   agree to + 제안: ~에 동의하다

② answer for: ~의 책임을 지다
   answer to: ~에 일치하다

③ apply for: ~에 지원하다
   apply to: ~에 적응하다

④ call on + 사람: ~을 방문하다
   call at + 장소: ~을 방문하다

⑤ call up: ~에게 전화를 걸다
   call for: ~를 데리러 가다, 요구하다

⑥ care for + 명사: 돌보다(긍정문), 좋아하다(의문문, 부정문)
   care to + 동사원형: ~하고 싶다

⑦ get on: ~에 타다
   get off: ~에서 내리다

⑧ hear of: 소문을 듣다
   hear from: 소식을 듣다

⑨ lay out: 지출하다, 설계하다
   lay up: 저축하다

⑩ look for: ~을 찾다
   look after: ~을 돌보다

⑪ look into: 조사하다
   look over: 훑어보다

⑫ look like: ~같이 보이다
   look on: ~을 방관하다

⑬ part from: (사람)과 헤어지다
   part with: (물건)을 내놓다, 팔아 버리다

⑭ pick out: 선택하다
   pick up: 줍다

⑮ put on: 입다
   put off: 연기하다, 벗다

⑯ run after: ~을 쫓다
   run away: 도망가다

⑰ make up: 화장하다
   make up for: 보충하다, 보상하다

⑱ wait for: ~을 기다리다
   wait on: 시중들다

2 〈형용사 + 전치사〉의 형태

① be angry at(about) + 사물:　~에 화를 내다
　 be angry with + 사람:　~에 화를 내다
② be anxious about:　~을 걱정하다
　 be anxious for:　~을 갈망하다
③ be familiar to + 사람:　~에게 잘 알려져 있다
　 be familiar with + 사물:　~을 잘 알고 있다
④ be good at:　~을 잘하다
　 be good for:　~에 좋다
⑤ be tired of:　~에 싫증나다
　 be tired with:　~으로 지치다
⑥ be concerned in(with):　~에 관계하다
　 be concerned about(for):　~을 고려하다

3 〈동사 + 명사 + 전치사〉의 형태

① find fault with:　비난하다
② give attention to:　~에 주의하다
③ keep company with:　~와 교제하다
④ make fun of:　~을 놀리다
⑤ make use of:　~을 이용하다
⑥ take advantage of:　~을 이용하다, ~을 속이다
⑦ take pride in　~을 자랑하다
⑧ take part in: :　~에 참가하다

4 〈동사 + 부사 + 전치사〉의 형태

① catch up with:　~을 따라잡다
② do away with:　~을 제거하다, ~을 그만두다
③ get along with:　~와 사이좋게 지내다
④ look down upon:　~을 멸시하다
⑤ look up to:　~을 존경하다
⑥ look forward to:　~을 학수고대하다
⑦ put up with:　참다
⑧ speak ill of:　~를 욕하다
⑨ speak well of:　~을 칭찬하다

5 〈형용사 + of〉의 형태

① be afraid of: ~을 두려워하다
② be ashamed of: ~을 부끄럽게 여기다
③ be aware of: ~을 알고 있다
④ be capable of: ~을 할 수 있다
⑤ be careful of: ~을 주의하다
⑥ be conscious of: ~을 알고 있다
⑦ be fond of: ~을 좋아하다
⑧ be full of: ~으로 가득 차다
⑨ be ignorant of: ~을 모르다
⑩ be proud of: ~을 자랑하다
⑪ be sure of: ~을 확신하다

6 〈형용사 + to〉의 형태

① be equal to: ~와 같다, ~을 견디어 내다
② be indifferent to: ~에 무관심하다
③ be liable to: ~하기 쉽다
④ be sensitive to: ~에 민감하다
⑤ be superior to: ~보다 우월하다
⑥ be inferior to: ~보다 열등하다
⑦ be thankful to + 사람: ~에게 감사를 하다 (be thankful for + 사물)
⑧ be true to: ~에 충실하다

7 〈형용사 + for, from〉의 형태

① be famous for: ~으로 유명하다
② be eager for: ~을 열망하다
③ be ready for: ~에 준비가 되어 있다
④ be responsible for: ~에 대하여 책임을 지고 있다
⑤ be suitable for: ~에 적합하다
⑥ be far from: 결코 ~이 아니다
⑦ be free from: ~이 없다
⑧ be different from: ~와 다르다
⑨ be absent from: 결석하다

Pattern Practice

1. I was surprised **at** him.

2. We were crying **over** the death of his father.

3. He died **from** smoking too much.

4. She died **of** cancer.

5. He went **on** an errand the day before yesterday.

6. The policeman **ran after** the robber.

7. He was killed **with** a gun.

8. She was killed **by** a robber.

9. Wine is made **from** grapes.

10. Grapes are made **into** wine.

11. They sell sugar **by** the pound.

12. He is **from** New York.

13. I will **call** you **up** this morning.

14. He **called on** me yesterday.

15. He **called at** my house last week.

16. You must **put off** your departure.

17. You had better **make use of** your chance.

18. Don't **speak ill of** her.

19. She **took pride in** her son.

20. We **are eager for** freedom.

연습문제

1. 다음 영문을 우리말로 옮기시오.

(1) I was surprised at her pale face. _____

(2) He wept over the death of his son. _____

(3) He is ill from smoking and drinking too much. _____

(4) She failed through her idleness. _____

(5) She died of cancer. _____

(6) He took cold with cold rain and wind. _____

(7) He sent for a doctor. _____

(8) My father went on a tour last year. _____

(9) Butter is made from milk. _____

(10) She is from Seoul. _____

(11) Would you care for coffee? _____

(12) You must care for children. _____

(13) She would like to wait on her grandmother. _____

(14) Don't make fun of me. _____

(15) I am ashamed of having been a thief. _____

2. 다음 문장을 영작하시오.

(1) 당신은 어디 출신입니까? _____

(2) 포도주는 포도로 만들어진다. _____

(3) 그녀는 자기 아들이 의사인 것을 자랑스러워한다. _____

(4) 당신은 다음 버스정류장에서 내려야 한다. _____

(5) 나는 오랫동안 걸어서 피곤하였다. _____

3. 다음 (　) 안에서 알맞은 말을 고르시오.

(1) I get up early (at, in) seven (on, in) the morning.

(2) I will wait for her (till, by) six in the evening.

(3) I will be back (till, by) six in the evening.

(4) He has lived in Seoul (for, during) ten years.

(5) He has lived in Seoul (from, since) last year.

(6) His father lived in New York from 2015 (to, till) 2018.

(7) His sister studied from morning (to, till) night.

(8) His father has lived in New York (from, since) 2017.

(9) He sat (between, among) his students.

(10) She swam (across, through) the river in summer.

(11) She traveled (across, through) the jungle.

(12) I was walking (along, through) the street.

(13) The earth goes (around, round) the sun.

(14) The old man sat (around, round) the table.

(15) The man walked (around, about) the street.

(16) She died (from, of) cancer last year.

(17) He died (from, of) overwork.

(18) She was killed (by, with) a knife.

(19) He was killed (by, with) a robber.

(20) Butter is made (from, of) milk.

(21) The desk is made (from, of) wood.

(22) Grapes are made (from, into) wine.

(23) She called (on, at) me yesterday.

(24) She called (on, at) my house yesterday.

(25) He is fond (for, of) my sister.

(26) He is absent (from, at) school today.

(27) She is tired (of, with) walking for a long time.

(28) She is tired (of, with) learning English.

(29) He is good (at, for) baseball.

(30) She called me (up, for) the other day.

4. 다음 ( ) 안에 알맞은 말을 써 넣으시오.

(1) He is listening ( ) music.

(2) This is the house ( ) he lives in.

(3) Do you know the boy whom she is fond ( )?

(4) I met him ( ) front of the building.

(5) She studied hard in spite ( ) being ill.

(6) She went to New York ( ) way of Hawaii.

(7) He went out ( ) a walk.

(8) We have lunch at school ( ) noon.

(9) We had a wonderful party ( ) Christmas last year.

(10) He arrived ( ) Incheon International Airport.

(11) You have to put ( ) your departure.

(12) She was afraid ( ) dogs.

(13) He is looking ( ) his friend among them.

(14) I put ( ) an overcoat in winter.

(15) We take ( ) our hats in the room.

5. 다음 문장에서 잘못된 곳이 있으면 바르게 고치시오.

(1) Please pick up it in front of him. _____

(2) I am looking forward to see her. _____

(3) I will stay in Seoul during a month. _____

(4) His father worked from morning to night. _____

(5) We had a good party at her birthday. _____

6. 다음 영문을 우리말로 옮기시오.

(1) The house on the hill is mine. _____

(2) There is a beautiful house on the hill. _____

(3) You had better get off at the next bus stop. _____

(4) I always get on the bus in front of his house. _____

중학 영어
기적의 영문법 1

해답

문장

연습문제   p.15

1. 다음 문장의 형식을 쓰고 우리말로 옮기시오.

(1) 그는 버스를 타고 학교에 간다. (1형식)

(2) 그는 선생님이 되었다. (2형식)

(3) 그는 집을 만들었다. (3형식)

(4) 그는 나에게 집을 만들어 주었다. (4형식)

(5) 그녀는 나를 선생님으로 만들었다. (5형식)

(6) 그녀는 어제 일찍 일어났다. (1형식)

(7) 그녀는 나를 행복하게 만들었다. (5형식)

(8) 그녀는 나에게 책 한 권을 사주었다. (3형식)

(9) 그녀는 나를 만나기를 원한다. (3형식)

(10) 그는 내가 그녀를 만나기를 원한다. (5형식)

(11) 그는 내가 책을 읽는 것을 보았다. (5형식)

(12) 그는 내가 책을 읽고 있는 것을 보았다. (5형식)

(13) 그는 나에게 몇 권의 책을 주었다. (4형식)

(14) 그녀는 책 읽는 것을 즐거워한다. (3형식)

(15) 그녀는 그가 현명하다고 생각한다. (3형식)

(16) 그녀는 무엇을 해야 할지 모른다. (3형식)

(17) 그녀는 내가 노래 부르는 것을 들었다. (5형식)

(18) 그녀는 내가 노래 부르도록 했다. (5형식)

(19) 그 속에 몇 권의 책들이 있다. (1형식)

(20) 그는 과학자가 되었다. (2형식)

2. 다음 문장을 영작하시오.

(1) I was at home yesterday.

(2) I was a doctor.

(3) I get up early in the morning.

(4) I want her to study.

(5) I saw her study.

(6) I saw her studying.

(7) I don't know what to do.

(8) I know that he is honest.

(9) I made him a box.

(10) I made him a doctor. *made = became: 되었다

연습문제   p.19

1. 다음 문장을 부정문으로 고치시오.

(1) I am not a good student.

(2) You are not a good student.

(3) He is not a good student.

(4) There is not a book on the desk.

(5) I don't have a good friend.

(6) You don't have a good friend.

(7) She doesn't have a good friend.

(8) She doesn't go to school, either.

(9) She didn't go to school, either.

(10) She didn't have any friends, either.

(11) He doesn't play baseball.

(12) He can not play baseball.

(13) He is not able to play baseball.

(14) He didn't want to go to school.

(15) He doesn't have to study hard.

2. 다음 문장을 의문문으로 고치시오.

(1) Am I a good student?

(2) Is my sister beautiful?

(3) Are my sisters beautiful?

(4) Was there a book on the desk, too?

(5) Is he reading a book?

(6) Does he read a book?

(7) Does he have any flowers?

(8) Does he have to stay here?

(9) Did he have any flowers?

(10) Does he go to church?

(11) Did he go to church?

(12) Does she play tennis well, too?

(13) Can she play tennis well, too?

(14) Is she able to play tennis well, too?

(15) Does she want to go to church?

연습문제   p.22

다음 (　) 안에 알맞은 낱말을 써 넣으시오.

(1) (I) (am)

(I'm) (a) (doctor)

(I) (am) (a) (doctor)

(2) (I'm) (not)

(I'm) (not) (a) (nurse)/(I'm)

(3) (he) (is)

(he's) (a) (farmer)

(he) (is) (a) (farmer)
(4) (she) (isn't)
　(she) (isn't) (a) (doctor)/(She's)
　(she) (is) (not) (a) (doctor)/(She's)
(5) (there) (is)
　(there) (is) (a) (book)
(6) (there) (aren't) (any)
　(there) (aren't) (any)
(7) (I) (do)
　(I) (have) (a) (book)
(8) (they) (don't)
　(they) (don't) (have) (many) (books)
(9) (she) (does)
　(she) (goes) (to) (school)
(10) (he) (didn't)
　(he) (didn't) (go) (to) (school)
(11) (I) (can)
　(I) (can) (speak) (English)

연습문제　　　　　　　　　　　p.24

다음 ( ) 안에 알맞은 낱말을 써 넣으시오.
(1) (who)　　　　　(2) (what)
(3) (who)　　　　　(4) (time)
(5) (day)　　　　　(6) (the) (date)
(7) (time)　　　　　(8) (When)
(9) (When)　　　　(10) (where)
(11) (Why)　　　　(12) (How)
(13) (Who)　　　　(14) (What)

연습문제　　　　　　　　　　　p.27

1. 다음 밑줄을 친 곳에 알맞은 부가의문문을 써 넣으시오.
(1) aren't you　　　(2) are you
(3) don't you　　　(4) do you
(5) can't you　　　(6) can you
(7) won't you　　　(8) will you
(9) isn't it　　　　(10) is it
(11) isn't he　　　(12) is he
(13) doesn't she　　(14) does she
(15) didn't he　　　(16) didn't she

(17) doesn't he　　(18) does she
(19) doesn't he　　(20) hasn't he
(21) will you　　　(22) will you
(23) shall we　　　(24) shall we
(25) wasn't he

2. 다음 문장을 영작하시오.
(1) She is happy, isn't she?
(2) It is fine today, isn't it?
(3) You are tired, aren't you?
(4) Your aren't ill, are you?
(5) You are sleepy, aren't you?

연습문제　　　　　　　　　　　p.32

1. 다음 두 문장을 연결하여 간접의문으로 만드시오.
(1) Do you know who she is?
(2) Who do you think he is?
(3) Do you know who likes you?
(4) Who do you think likes you?
(5) Do you know who loved you?
(6) Who do you think loved you?
(7) Do you know where he lives?
(8) Where do you think he lives?
(9) Do you know when she started?
(10) When do you think she started?

2. 다음 문장을 명령문으로 만드시오.
(1) Go home quickly.
(2) Don't go home quickly.
(3) Be kind to him.
(4) Let me know his name.
(5) Let him know my name.

3. 다음 문장을 감탄문으로 만드시오.
(1) How beautiful she is!
(2) What a beautiful girl she is!
(3) How nice this house is!
(4) What a nice house this is!
(5) How fast the rabbit runs!

1. 다음 ( ) 안에 밑줄 친 구의 종류를 써 넣으시오.

(1) 부사구
(2) 형용사구
(3) 명사구
(4) 형용사구
(5) 장소 부사구, 부사구
(6) 장소 부사구, 시간 부사구
(7) 시간 부사구, 시간 부사구
(8) 명사구
(9) 명사구
(10) 장소 부사구

2. 다음 ( ) 안에 밑줄 친 절의 종류를 써 넣으시오.

(1) 명사절
(2) 형용사절
(3) 형용사절
(4) 명사절
(5) 부사절

1. 다음 문장을 ( ) 안의 지시대로 바꿔 쓰시오.

(1) Are there any books on the desk?
(2) He didn't go to school at seven.
(3) How beautiful she is!
(4) Be kind to others.
(5) I don't know where he lives.

2. 다음 ( ) 안에 문장의 형식을 써 넣고 우리말로 옮기시오.

(1) 그는 버스로 학교에 간다. (1형식)
(2) 그녀는 그를 행복하게 해주었다. (5형식)
(3) 너는 그녀가 서울을 언제 떠날지 아니? (3형식)
(4) 그녀는 나에게 약간의 꽃을 보냈다. (4형식)
(5) 그녀는 매우 아름다워 보인다. (2형식)

3. 다음 ( ) 안에 알맞은 말을 써 넣으시오.

(1) (isn't it)
(2) (doesn't he)
(3) (will you)
(4) (What)

(5) (I) (didn't). (studied)

1. 다음 영문을 우리말로 옮기시오.

(1) 가방 안에 공책 한 권이 있다.
(2) 가방 안에 약간의 공책이 있다.
(3) 문(필력)은 무보다 강하다.
(4) 나의 학급은 큰 학급이다.
(5) 우리 반은 모두 부지런하다.
(6) 나는 브라운 성을 가진 한 아가씨를 만났다.
(7) 셰익스피어와 같은 극작가는 뉴턴과 같은 과학자가 될 수 없다.
(8) 행복이 마음속에 있으므로 나는 행복하다.
(9) 개는 영리한 동물이다.
(10) 공원에는 많은 사람들이 있다.
(11) 아시아에는 많은 민족이 있다.
(12) 김 양은 미인이다.
(13) 우리 반에는 김 씨 성을 가진 사람이 많다.
(14) 나는 안경을 하나 샀다.
(15) 나는 아저씨의 농장에 가기를 원한다.

2. 다음 문장을 영작하시오.

(1) I bought a cake of soap.
(2) I want to be a Newton.
(3) He wants to go to America.
(4) My family are all diligent.
(5) Would you like a cup of coffee?
= Would you like to have a cup of coffee?

3. 다음 ( ) 안에 알맞은 말을 써 넣으시오.

(1) glass
(2) cup
(3) pieces
(4) cakes
(5) sheet

4. 다음 ( ) 안에서 알맞은 말을 고르시오.

(1) is
(2) are

(3) are

(4) are

(5) are

5. 다음 문장에서 잘못된 곳을 바르게 고치시오.

(1) father → Father

(2) waters → water

(3) Newton of Korea → a Newton in Korea

(4) Mr. Tom → Tom

(5) kind → kindness

6. 다음 밑줄 친 명사의 종류를 써 넣으시오.

(1) 보통명사

(2) 물질명사

(3) 군집명사

(4) 보통명사

(5) 고유명사

연습문제   p.55

1. 다음 영문을 우리말로 옮기시오.

(1) 나의 형은 양들을 지켜본다.

(2) 나는 안경 한 개를 샀다.

(3) 나는 시인과 선생님을 만났다.

(4) 나는 시인인 선생님을 만났다.

(5) 그는 아저씨 집에 간다.

(6) 태양은 열과 빛을 스스로 발산한다.

(7) 한국은 경치로 유명하다.

(8) 그는 열 살 난 소년이다.

(9) 그 배는 그 승무원과 승객들과 더불어 가라앉았다.

(10) 나는 아버지의 옛 친구 한 분을 만났다.

(11) 고양이는 매우 영리하다.

(12) 고양이들은 매우 영리하다.

(13) 바구니 안에 사과 하나가 있다.

(14) 바구니 안에 약간의 사과가 있다.

(15) 나는 내 친구를 만났다.

2. 다음 문장을 영작하시오.

(1) I met an old friend of my mother's.

(2) He is twelve years old.

(3) There is a book on the desk.

(4) I went to my uncle's.

(5) She met her friend.

3. 다음 명사의 복수형을 쓰시오.

(1) books   (2) babies

(3) boys   (4) girls

(5) benches   (6) knives

(7) roofs   (8) geese

(9) men   (10) boy−friends

4. 다음 복수형의 어미 −(e)s의 발음을 [s], [z], [iz]로 구별하시오.

(1) [s]   (2) [iz]

(3) [z]   (4) [iz]

(5) [s]   (6) [iz]

(7) [z]   (8) [z]

(9) [iz]   (10) [z]

(11) [s]   (12) [s]

(13) [iz]   (14) [z]

(15) [iz]

5. 다음 문장에서 잘못된 곳을 바르게 고치시오.

(1) I met a friend of my father's.

(2) He went to his uncle's.

(3) The boy's teacher is kind.

(4) This book of my father's is very interesting.

(5) The roof of my house is green.

6. 다음 각 단어의 반대되는 단어를 쓰시오.

(1) mother   (2) brother

(3) uncle   (4) woman

(5) princess   (6) girl−friend

(7) maid−servant   (8) lioness

(9) niece   (10) cow

종합문제   p.58

1. 다음 문장을 복수형으로 고친 것 중 잘못된 곳을 바르게 고치시오.

(1) a knives → knives

(2) babys → babies

(3) friend → friends

(4) milks → milk

2. 다음 문장에서 잘못된 곳을 바르게 고치시오.

(1) the boys's book → the boys' books

(2) the car's color → the color of the car

(3) my father's a car → my father's car

(4) Tom and Mary's books → Tom's and Mary's books

(5) five-years-old girl → five-year-old girl

(6) is → are

3. 다음 한글의 뜻을 영어로 쓰시오.

(1) my friend

(2) my father's friend

(3) a friend of my father's

(4) Tom's friend

(5) the legs of the desk

(6) today's paper

 03 관사

연습문제   p.65

1. 다음 영문을 우리말로 옮기시오.

(1) 나는 운동장에서 소년을 보았다. 그 소년은 훌륭한 테니스 선수였다.

(2) 1년은 12달이 있다.

(3) 어떤 신사가 어제 너를 만나러 왔다.

(4) 그들은 같은 사업을 한다.

(5) 나는 하루에 세끼를 먹는다.

(6) 여우는 교활한 동물이다.

(7) 1월은 연중 첫 번째 달이다.

(8) 그녀는 나의 손을 잡았다.

(9) 부자들이 반드시 행복한 것은 아니다.

(10) 그녀는 바이올린을 매우 잘 연주한다.

2. 다음 ( ) 안에 a, an, the를 써 넣으시오. 필요 없는 곳에는 ×표를 하시오.

(1) a   (2) an

(3) a   (4) ×

(5) the   (6) The, the

(7) the   (8) the

(9) The   (10) ×

(11) the   (12) ×

(13) ×, the

연습문제   p.70

1. 다음 ( ) 안에서 알맞은 관사를 고르시오.

(1) The   (2) the

(3) an   (4) a

(5) an   (6) The Han River

(7) the   (8) the

2. 다음 영문을 우리말로 옮기시오.

(1) 나는 선생임이자 시인인 사람을 만났다.

(2) 나는 선생님과 시인을 만났다.

(3) 설탕은 파운드로 팔린다.

(4) 그는 나의 머리를 쳤다.

(5) 노인들은 혼자 산에 갈 수 없다.

(6) 부모님은 두 분 다 살아 계신다.

(7) 그녀는 버스로 학교에 다닌다.

(8) 그는 승용차로 학교에 다닌다.

3. 다음 문장에서 잘못된 곳을 바르게 고치시오.

(1) mother → Mother or his mother

(2) a president → president

(3) How a pretty girl → How pretty

(4) so a tall boy → so tall a boy

 04 대명사

연습문제   p.79

1. 다음 ( ) 안에서 알맞은 것을 고르시오.

(1) her

(2) hers

(3) she

(4) me, him

(5) mine

2. 다음 영문에서 it의 용법을 쓰고 우리말로 옮기시오.

(1) 여기서 너의 집까지 거리가 얼마니? (거리)

(2) 겨울에는 춥다. (날씨)

(3) 영어를 배우는 것은 어렵다. (가주어)

(4) 나는 영어를 공부하는 것이 쉽다고 생각한다. (

가목적어)

(5) 내가 그녀를 공원에서 만난 것은 어제였다. (
강조용법)

3. 밑줄 친 부분을 하나의 대명사로 고치시오.
(1) We
(2) You
(3) They
(4) We
(5) They

4. 다음 (   ) 안에 알맞은 말을 써 넣으시오.
(1) We
(2) day
(3) date
(4) It
(5) himself

5. 다음을 영어로 옮기시오.
(1) We have much rain in summer.
(2) You should respect your neighbors.
(3) Tom did his homework for himself.
(4) This book is his.
(5) This is his school.

연습문제　　　　　　　　　　　p.84

1. 다음 영문을 우리말로 옮기시오.
(1) 이것은 나의 책이다.
(2) 이 책은 나의 것이다.
(3) 서울의 겨울은 일본의 겨울보다 춥다.
(4) 나는 오늘 아침 승용차로 학교에 갈 것이다.
(5) 나는 그날 아침 학교에서 그를 만났다.
(6) 요즘 그 도시에는 많은 사람들이 있다.
(7) 부지런하지 않은 사람은 성공할 수 없다.
(8) 토끼의 귀는 개의 귀보다 더 길다.
(9) 그 당시에는 텔레비전이 없었다.
(10) 개와 여우가 있는데; 후자는 교활하고, 전자
는 충실하다.

2. 다음 문장을 영작하시오.
(1) That car is not good.
(2) That is not a good car.

(3) I am going to get up early tomorrow morning.
(4) How have you been these days?
(5) I am going to study English this week.

연습문제　　　　　　　　　　　p.89

1. 다음 영문을 우리말로 옮기시오.
(1) 사람은 약속을 지켜야 한다.
(2) 나는 두 명의 형제가 있다. 한 명은 선생님이
고, 다른 한 명은 의사이다.
(3) 나는 많은 책이 있다. 하나는 쉽고 그 나머지
는 쉽지 않다.
(4) 나는 많은 책을 가지고 있다. 어떤 것은 쉽고,
어떤 것은 쉽지 않다.
(5) 나는 이 브러시가 싫습니다. 다른 하나를 보여
주시겠습니까?
(6) 당신은 정원에 약간의 꽃이 있습니까?
(7) 나는 정원에 약간의 꽃이 있다.
(8) 나는 정원에 한 송이의 꽃도 없다.
(9) 커피 좀 하시겠습니까
(10) 돈이 좀 있으면 그에게 좀 빌려 주세요.
(11) 톰과 메리는 서로를 도왔다.
(12) 그들은 서로를 도왔다.
(13) 당신과 그 사람 중 하나는 나쁘다.
(14) 당신과 나 중 어느 쪽도 나쁘지 않다.
(15) 그들 중 둘 다 나쁘지는 않다.

2. 다음 문장을 영작하시오.
(1) Mom, may I have another egg?
(2) Would you like some milk?
(3) I don't have any money.
(4) He and she love each other.
(5) The rich are not always happy.

3. 다음 (   ) 안에서 알맞은 말을 고르시오.
(1) are	(2) is
(3) are	(4) is
(5) are	(6) is
(7) is	(8) are
(9) is	(10) is
(11) is	(12) are

4. 다음 (   ) 안에 알맞은 말을 써 넣으시오.

(1) one's   (2) one
(3) it   (4) the, other
(5) another   (6) other
(7) for   (8) by
(9) another   (10) another, third
(11) others   (12) some
(13) any

(9) How   (10) Why

4. 다음 두 문장을 연결하여 간접의문문을 만드시오.

(1) Do you know who met the lady?
(2) Who do you think met the lady?
(3) Do you know where he lives?
(4) Where do you think he went?
(5) When do you think he will start?

연습문제   p.94

1. 다음 영문을 우리말로 옮기시오.

(1) 이것과 저것 중에서 당신은 어느 것을 더 좋아합니까?
(2) 이것은 누구의 가방입니까?
(3) 이 가방은 누구의 것입니까?
(4) 그는 무엇을 가지기를 원합니까?
(5) 그녀는 무슨 책을 가지기를 원합니까?
(6) 너는 저 자동차를 언제 샀니?
(7) 나는 그가 서울을 언제 떠날지 모른다.
(8) 오늘은 내가 태어난 날이다.
(9) 나의 어머니는 나의 남동생이 태어났을 때 기뻐했다.
(10) 여기서 당신의 학교까지 얼마나 멉니까?
(11) 학교까지 가는 데 얼마나 걸립니까?
(12) 너는 어제 왜 결석했니?
(13) 너 어디 가니?
(14) 너는 이 책을 어디에서 읽을 작정이니?
(15) 너는 서울을 언제 떠날 거니?

2. 다음 문장을 영작하시오.

(1) Where do you live?
(2) When is she going to leave?
(3) Why were you late yesterday?
(4) What does she want?
(5) This is the house where I was born.

3. 다음 두 문장의 뜻이 같도록 (   ) 안에 알맞은 말을 써 넣으시오.

(1) Where   (2) What
(3) Who   (4) What
(5) Who   (6) Who
(7) Whom   (8) Whose

연습문제   p.105

1. 다음 두 문장을 관계대명사를 써서 한 문장으로 만드시오.

(1) This is the man who teaches us English.
(2) This is the man whose son is a doctor.
(3) This is the man whom I met yesterday.
(4) This is the book which is written by him.
(5) This is the book which I bought in Seoul.
(6) This is the book whose cover is black.
    = This is the book of which the cover is black.
    = This is the book the cover of which is black.
(7) The woman who teaches us English is happy.
(8) The woman whose son is a doctor is happy.
(9) The woman whom I met yesterday is happy.
(10) The book which is written by him is good.
(11) The book whose cover is black is good.
(12) The book which I bought in Seoul is good.
(13) This is the first man that taught me English.
(14) This is the wisest woman that I know.
(15) This is the only money that I have.

2. 다음 영문을 우리말로 옮기시오.

(1) 나는 많은 책을 읽는 그 학생을 좋아한다.
(2) 내가 슈퍼마켓에서 만났던 숙녀는 나의 선생님이다.
(3) 이분은 하와이에서 살아온 최초의 그 한국인이다.
(4) 나는 아버지가 의사인 그 소년을 안다.
(5) 지붕이 빨간 그 집을 보아라.
(6) 나는 표지가 검은 책을 찾고 있는 중이다.
(7) 그는 시인이 쓴 책을 샀다.

(8) 나는 아버지가 작년에 나에게 사준 바로 그 시계를 잃어버렸다.

(9) 나는 방과 후 같이 놀 친구가 없다.

(10) 그녀가 쓴 그 책은 매우 재미있다.

(11) 나는 네가 말한 것을 이해할 수 없다.

(12) 자기 아이들을 사랑하지 않는 부모는 없다.

(13) 그녀는 많은 학생이 있다, 그런데 그들은 부지런하다.

(14) 나는 그 책을 읽을 수 없다, 왜냐하면 그것은 너무 어렵기 때문이다.

(15) 이것은 내가 살기를 원하는 그 집이다.

3. 다음 문장을 영작하시오.

(1) This is the book which I like.

(2) This is the woman who teaches us English.

(3) The book which I like is easy.

(4) The man who teaches us English is my father.

(5) This is the man whose son is a doctor.

4. 다음 ( ) 안에서 알맞은 관계대명사를 고르시오.

(1) whose	(2) who
(3) whom	(4) which
(5) whose	(6) which
(7) that	(8) that
(9) that	(10) that
(11) that	(12) that
(13) that	(14) that
(15) which	(16) that
(17) that	(18) whose
(19) that	(20) but

5. 다음 ( ) 안에 알맞은 관계대명사를 써 넣으시오.

(1) whose	(2) who
(3) whom	(4) whom
(5) whom	(6) that
(7) which	(8) whose
(9) which	(10) what
(11) what	(12) but
(13) that	(14) what
(15) that	(16) as
(17) that	(18) who
(19) which	(20) which

종합문제 p.113

1. 다음 영문을 우리말로 옮기시오.

(1) 이곳은 내가 태어난 마을이다.

(2) 이곳은 부산이다, 그런데 거기서 내가 태어났다.

(3) 이곳은 내가 태어난 마을이다.

(4) 오늘은 내가 태어난 날이다.

(5) 오늘은 9월 16일이다, 그런데 그때 나는 태어났다.

(6) 이것이 내가 너를 싫어하는 이유이다.

(7) 이것이 내가 집을 건축한 방법이다.

2. 다음 문장을 영작하시오.

(1) Do you know the house where she was born?

(2) I can not tell you the reason why I was absent yesterday.

(3) Can you tell me the day when you will leave Seoul?

3. 다음 두 문장의 뜻이 같도록 ( ) 안에 알맞은 말을 써 넣어라.

(1) (and) (there)

(2) (and) (then)

(3) (in) (which)

(4) (for) (which)

(5) (in) (which)

4. 다음 ( ) 안에 알맞은 관계대명사와 관계부사를 써 넣어라.

(1) which

(2) where

(3) what

(4) whom

(5) that

PART 05 형용사

연습문제 p.119

1. 다음 영문을 우리말로 옮기시오.

(1) 그녀는 무엇을 읽기를 원합니까?

(2) 그녀는 무슨 책을 읽기를 원합니까?

(3) 이 아이는 행복한 소녀이다.

(4) 이 소녀는 매우 행복하다.

(5) 나는 이 소녀를 행복하게 해 주었다.

(6) 그는 사랑스러운 소녀를 사랑한다.

(7) 그녀는 참 어리석구나!

(8) 나의 아버지의 생일 파티는 굉장한 것이었다.

(9) 그는 10년 동안 시각 장애인들과 청각 장애인
들을 가르쳐왔다.

(10) 영국의 현 여왕은 엘리자베스이다.

(11) 엘리자베스 여왕은 회의에 참석 중이다.

(12) 나의 여동생은 개를 무서워한다.

(13) 나는 찬 것을 마시기를 원한다.

(14) 그것은 매우 흥미진진한 경기였다.

(15) 모두 그 경기를 보고 무척 열광적이었다.

2. 다음 문장을 영작하시오.

(1) She is a beautiful girl.

(2) The girl is beautiful.

(3) I think the girl beautiful.

(4) I want to see what is beautiful.

(5) The girl has some books.

연습문제　　　　　　　　　　　p.129

1. 다음 명사의 형용사형을 쓰시오.

(1) sunny　　　　　　(2) friendly

(3) cloudy　　　　　　(4) English

(5) Korean　　　　　　(6) lovely

(7) foolish　　　　　　(8) rainy

(9) French　　　　　　(10) Japanese

2. 다음 (   ) 안에 형용사의 비교급과 최상급을 써 넣으시오.

(1) better, best

(2) bigger, biggest

(3) cleverer, cleverest

(4) more, most

(5) prettier, prettiest

(6) less, least

(7) more famous, most famous

(8) larger, largest

(9) older, oldest

(10) worse, worst

3. 다음 숫자를 영어로 쓰시오.

(1) two　　　　　　　(2) twelve

(3) twenty　　　　　　(4) four

(5) fourteen　　　　　(6) forty

(7) five　　　　　　　(8) fifteen

(9) fifty　　　　　　　(10) thirty-one

(11) second　　　　　(12) twelfth

(13) twentieth　　　　(14) fourth

(15) fourteenth　　　　(16) fortieth

(17) fifth　　　　　　(18) fifteenth

(19) fiftieth　　　　　(20) thirty-first

(21) eighty-two　　　(22) eighty-second

(23) nine　　　　　　(24) ninth

(25) nineteen　　　　(26) nineteenth

(27) one hundred　　(28) one hundredth

(29) one thousand

(30) three hundred (and) twenty-one million,
six hundred (and) fifty-four thousand, nine
hundred (and) eighty-seven

4. 다음을 영어로 쓰시오.

(1) a half

(2) nineteen ninety-nine

(3) September sixteenth (the sixteenth of September)

(4) eight five five five [ou] five two

(5) three-fourths

(6) nineteen [ou] six

(7) three point one, four

(8) two fifteen (= a quarter after two)

5. 다음 (   ) 안에서 알맞은 것을 고르시오.

(1) many　　　　　　(2) much

(3) a little　　　　　(4) a few

(5) a lot of　　　　　(6) much

(7) many　　　　　　(8) a lot of

(9) few　　　　　　　(10) little

6. 다음 (   ) 안에서 알맞은 것을 고르시오.

(1) are

(2) is

(3) exciting

(4) alive

(5) little, a little

7. 다음 문장에서 잘못된 곳을 바르게 고치시오.

(1) asleep → sleeping

(2) Two my kind → My two kind

(3) cold something → something cold

(4) two the → the two

(5) He is pleasant to come home early. → It is pleasant for him to come home early.

연습문제　　　　　　　　　　　p.136

1. 다음 영문을 우리말로 옮기시오.

(1) 그는 나만큼 강하다.

(2) 그는 나의 동생만큼 강하지 않다.

(3) 그는 나보다 더 강하다.

(4) 그 숙녀는 나의 누이보다 더 예쁘다.

(5) 그 숙녀는 나의 어머니보다 덜 예쁘다.

(6) 그는 나만큼 많은 책을 가지고 있다.

(7) 그는 자기 반에서 가장 강한 소년이다.

(8) 당신은 커피와 우유 중에서 어느 것을 더 좋아하세요?

(9) 잭은 둘 중에서 더 크다.

(10) 잭은 톰보다 두 살 더 많다.

(11) 이 연필은 저 연필보다 세 배 길다.

(12) 높이 올라가면 갈수록 더 추워진다.

(13) 나는 우유보다 커피를 더 좋아한다.

(14) 나는 그녀보다 너를 더 좋아한다.

(15) 그녀보다 내가 너를 더 좋아한다.

(16) 나는 겨우 10달러만을 가지고 있다.

(17) 점점 더워지고 있다.

(18) 나는 10달러나 가지고 있다.

(19) 톰은 반에서 다른 소년보다 더 키가 크다.

(20) 톰은 반에서 가장 키가 큰 소년이다.

2. 다음 (　) 안에서 알맞은 것을 고르시오.

(1) older　　　　　(2) elder

(3) taller　　　　　(4) oldest

(5) than　　　　　(6) to

(7) young　　　　(8) younger

(9) in　　　　　　(10) of

(11) cleverer　　　(12) better

(13) more　　　　(14) much

(15) colder

3. 다음 두 문장의 내용이 같아지도록 (　) 안에 알맞은 말을 써 넣으시오.

(1) less

(2) very

(3) only

(4) most

(5) other

4. 다음 문장의 내용과 같아지도록 (　) 안에 알맞은 말을 써 넣으시오.

(1) (any) (other)

(2) (as)

(3) (larger)

(4) (of) (all)

5. 다음 문장의 밑줄 친 부분을 구별하여 우리말로 옮기시오.

(1) a most = 매우

(2) the most = 가장

(3) most = 대부분의

(4) no more than = only = 단지

(5) no less than = as much as = ～만큼이나

(6) not more than = at most = 기껏해야

(7) not less than = at least = 적어도

(8) be superior to = ～보다 월등하다

(9) be inferior to = ～보다 못하다

(10) as good as = ～와 다름없다

6. 다음 영문을 우리말로 옮기시오.

(1) He is as tall as I.

(2) He is taller than I.

(3) She is not so beautiful as I.

(4) She is the tallest girl in her class.

(5) She is the most beautiful lady of them.

종합문제　　　　　　　　　　　p.139

1. 다음 (　) 안에서 알맞은 것을 고르시오.

197

(1) she, her
(2) she
(3) as many
(4) as much
(5) better

2. 다음 ( ) 안의 형용사를 알맞은 형으로 고쳐 쓰시오.
   (1) most diligent
   (2) prettier
   (3) more
   (4) less
   (5) better

3. 다음 숫자를 읽으시오.
   (1) two hundred (and) twenty-two million, two hundred (and) twenty-two thousand, two hundred (and) twenty-two
   (2) ① two ten
      ② ten (minutes) after (past) two (o'lock)
   (3) ① two thirty
      ② half after (past) two
   (4) ① September sixteenth
      ② the sixteenth of September
   (5) seventy-seven
   (6) one hundred (and) seven
   (7) two thousand

4. 다음에서 잘못된 곳을 바르게 고치시오.
   (1) bigger - biggest
   (2) prettier - prettiest
   (3) more useful - most useful
   (4) worse - worst

PART 06 부사

연습문제   p.145

1. 다음 영문을 우리말로 옮기시오.
   (1) 나는 어제 학교에 늦었다.
   (2) 그 전철은 10분이 늦다.
   (3) 우리는 늦가을에 소풍을 갔습니다.
   (4) 고 링컨 대통령은 미국에서 가장 위대한 사람

이었습니다.
   (5) 그녀는 어제 늦게 잤습니다.
   (6) 밤에 너무 늦게 외출하지 마라.
   (7) 너는 요즈음 영어에 흥미가 있니?
   (8) 나는 영어가 어렵다고 생각한다.
   (9) 나는 딱딱한 아이스크림이 먹고 싶다.
   (10) 여러분은 젊어서 항상 열심히 공부해야 한다.
   (11) 나는 그가 말한 것을 거의 이해할 수가 없다.
   (12) 그는 항상 큰 목소리로 이야기한다.
   (13) 제트기 한 대가 하늘 높이 날아가고 있다.
   (14) 당신을 오랫동안 보지 못했습니다. (오랜만에 뵙겠습니다.)
   (15) 나의 할아버지는 매우 오래 살고 계십니다.

2. 다음 문장을 영작하시오.
   (1) I can teach you English easily.
   (2) Get up early in the morning.
   (3) He studies English hard at home.
   (4) Why are you late this morning?
   (5) I was ill yesterday.

3. 다음 ( ) 안에 각 단어의 부사형을 쓰시오.
   (1) kindly   (2) easily
   (3) usually   (4) fully
   (5) truly   (6) slowly
   (7) late   (8) happily
   (9) daily   (10) fast
   (11) beautifully   (12) early
   (13) monthly   (14) much
   (15) enough   (16) carefully
   (17) gently   (18) long
   (19) high   (20) quickly

4. 다음 ( ) 안에서 알맞은 말을 고르시오.
   (1) well   (2) pretty
   (3) late   (4) easy
   (5) easily   (6) hardly
   (7) hard   (8) lately
   (9) highly   (10) high

5. 다음 문장의 밑줄 친 부분에 유의하여 우리말로 옮기시오.
   (1) 당신은 언제 서울을 떠납니까?

(2) 너는 그가 언제 서울을 떠날 거라고 생각하니?

(3) 나는 젊었을 때, 야구하기를 좋아했다.

(4) 오늘은 그가 태어난 날이다.

(5) 너의 생일이 언제니?

연습문제   p.151

1. 다음 영문을 우리말로 옮기시오.

1. 어린애라도 그것을 할 수 있다.

2. 너는 그 밖에 어떤 것을 원하니?

3. 그녀는 공원에서 천천히 걷는다.

4. 그녀는 영어를 매우 느리게 이야기한다.

5. 다행히도 그는 죽지 않았다.

6. 그는 행복하게 죽지 않았다.

7. 그는 매일 아침 전철로 학교에 간다.

8. 옛날 영국에 '아서'란 이름의 왕이 살았다.

9. 그는 보통 학교에 지각한다.

10. 그는 방과 후에는 보통 야구를 한다.

11. 내가 공부하는 동안에는 라디오를 좀 꺼 주십시오.

12. 그것을 좀 집어 주십시오.

13. 어제 나는 저녁 7시에 집에 갔다.

14. 나는 어제 9시 30분에 교회에 갔다.

15. 그녀는 오후 다섯 시에는 항상 슈퍼마켓에 간다.

2. 다음 문장을 영작하시오.

(1) She walks very fast.

(2) She speaks English very slowly.

(3) I walk to school every morning.

(4) He always reads a book.

(5) He is always busy.

연습문제   p.155

1. 다음 영문을 우리말로 옮기시오.

(1) 책상 위에 책이 한 권 있다.

(2) 책이 많이 있다.

(3) 거기에는 책이 많이 있다.

(4) 여기에는 많은 우유가 있다.

(5) 여기에 많은 우유가 있다.

(6) 이것은 매우 흥미 있는 경기이다.

(7) 스타디움에 있는 사람들은 매우 흥분되어 있다.

(8) 그녀는 자기 아들을 다시 보게 되어서 매우 기뻐합니다.

(9) 그녀는 개를 매우 무서워한다.

(10) 너는 숙제를 벌써 다 했니?

(11) 너는 그 일을 벌써 다 끝냈니?

(12) 그는 그 건물을 이미 지었다.

(13) 나는 아직 나의 숙제를 다 하지 않았다.

(14) 나는 2년 전에 런던에서 그를 만났다.

(15) 그녀는 지난달부터 아프다.

2. 다음 문장을 영작하시오.

(1) I met him two weeks ago.

(2) Here are many oranges.

(3) She is much interested in music.

(4) This book is very interesting.

(5) I have not finished my homework yet.

3. 다음 ( ) 안에서 알맞은 말을 고르시오.

(1) very

(2) much

(3) very

(4) much

(5) very

(6) very

(7) much

(8) ago

(9) since

(10) already

(11) yet

(12) before

(13) much

(14) No

(15) No

4. 다음 ( ) 안에 문장이 맞으면 ○, 틀리면 ×를 써 넣으시오.

(1) ○

(2) ×

(3) ○

(4) ○

(5) ×

(6) ○

(7) ×

(8) ○

(9) ×

(10) ○

연습문제   p.159

1. 다음 영문을 우리말로 옮기시오.

(1) 그도 역시 바이올린을 연주한다.

(2) 그는 테니스를 잘 한다. 나 역시 그렇다.

(3) 그녀도 역시 책을 읽고 있다.

(4) 그녀는 책을 읽고 있다. 나 역시 그렇다.

(5) 그녀도 역시 피아노를 칠 줄 모른다.

(6) 그녀는 테니스를 잘 못한다. 나 역시 그렇다.

(7) 그는 야구를 하지 않는다. 나 역시 그렇다.

(8) 나는 거의 학교에 지각을 하지 않는다.

(9) 그녀는 너무 나이 들어서 산책 나가지 못한다.

(10) 이 책은 너무 어려워서 그는 읽을 수 없다.

(11) 이 책은 너무 어려워서 그는 읽을 수 없다.

(12) 그녀는 혼자서는 학교까지 거의 걸어갈 수 없다.

(13) 그 집은 이미 지어졌다.

(14) 그는 그 경기가 흥미진진하다고 생각했다.

(15) 나는 그가 정직한 사람이었다고 믿었다.

2. 다음 문장을 영작하시오.

(1) His mother cooks well, too.

(2) I can not play the piano, either.

(3) I go to church with my mother every Sunday.

(4) He is too old to work.

(5) He hardly reads a book.

3. 다음 두 문장의 내용이 같아지도록 (　) 안에 알맞은 말을 써 넣으시오.

(1) (So)

(2) (Neither)

(3) (So)

(4) (Neither)

(5) (So) (that) (can) (not)

(6) (so) (that) (he) (it)

(7) (seldom, scarcely)

(8) (that) (he)

(9) (so)

(10) (hardly)

4. 다음 우리말을 참고하여 (　) 안에 알맞은 말을 써 넣으시오.

(1) (too) (to)

(2) (so) (that)

(3) (So)

(4) (So)

(5) (Neither)

종합문제　　　　　　　　p.161

1. 다음 영문을 우리말로 옮기시오.

(1) 당신은 그가 지금 살고 있는 도시를 압니까?

(2) 나의 할머니는 아직 살아 계십니다.

(3) 내 친구는 최근에 일본에서 돌아왔다.

(4) 나는 졸업 후에 제인을 거의 볼 수 없다.

(5) 이 책은 너무 어려워서 읽을 수 없다.

2. 다음 문장을 영작하시오.

(1) When are you going go leave Seoul?

(2) I am going to leave Seoul in May.

(3) Why are you late for school everyday?

(4) He is so poor that he can not go to university.

(5) I studied hard at school.

3. 다음 (　) 안에서 알맞은 것을 고르시오.

(1) well

(2) easy

(3) very

(4) yet

(5) ago

4. 다음 문장에서 잘못된 곳이 있으면 바르게 고치시오.

(1) 맞음

(2) Please pick them up.

(3) He has been to New York lately.

(4) She learned English easily.

(5) This blouse looks good.

PART 07 전치사

연습문제　　　　　　　　p.170

1. 다음 영문을 우리말로 옮기시오.

(1) 그녀는 음악을 공부하러 이탈리아에 가버렸다.

(2) 그 상점에 있는 자동차는 한국에서 만들어졌다.

(3) 백화점에는 많은 한국제 상품들이 있다.

(4) 그녀는 파티에서 영어 말하기를 두려워한다.

(5) 내가 공부를 하고 있는 동안에는 라디오를 꺼주십시오.

(6) 그는 결혼한 이래 줄곧 행복했다.

(7) 그는 그 후 내내 행복했다.

(8) 그는 그녀와 결혼한 후에 줄곧 행복했다.

(9) 그녀는 누구를 찾고 있습니까

(10) 나는 야구를 같이 할 친구가 많이 있다.

(11) 그 배는 거대한 바위 뒤에서 나타났다.

(12) 거리 한가운데 경찰관이 있다.

(13) 나는 일요일 전부터 중국어 배우기를 시작했다.

(14) 오늘 신문에 의하면, 부산에는 대화재가 있었다.

(15) 그는 자기 아버지의 도움 덕분에 성공했다.

2. 다음 문장을 영작하시오.

(1) Because of the rain, we can not go on a picnic.

(2) My sister is playing with her friends in the room.

(3) I watch TV after dinner.

(4) I have no house to live in.

(5) Please pick up the pencil.

연습문제   p.176

1. 다음 영문을 우리말로 옮기시오.

(1) 나는 그를 저녁 6시까지 기다리겠다.

(2) 나는 저녁 6시까지 돌아오겠다.

(3) 나는 나의 여름방학 기간 중에 바다에 갈 것이다.

(4) 밤새도록 비가 왔다.

(5) 그녀는 일 년 후에 돌아올 것이다.

(6) 그는 태평양을 비행 횡단한 최초의 한국인이다.

(7) 그들은 정글을 통과했다.

(8) 내가 거리를 걷고 있는 동안, 나는 그녀를 만났다.

(9) 막차가 부산을 향해서 떠났다.

(10) 아이들이 탁자 주위에 앉았다.

(11) 지구가 태양 주위를 돈다.

(12) 그는 제인과 메리 사이에 앉았다.

(13) 나는 그들 중에서 그를 뽑았다.

(14) 그들은 하루 종일 돌아다녔다.

(15) 나는 극장 안에서 그녀 뒤에 앉았다.

2. 다음 문장을 영작하시오.

(1) There are two books on the table.

(2) I saw an airplane flying over the mountain.

(3) He told me to stand up.

(4) I came home at ten at night.

(5) He has lived at Sillim-dong in Seoul for ten years.

연습문제   p.183

1. 다음 영문을 우리말로 옮기시오.

(1) 나는 그녀의 창백한 얼굴을 보고 깜짝 놀랐다.

(2) 그는 자기 아들의 죽음에 울었다.

(3) 그는 담배를 너무 많이 피우고 술을 너무 많이 마셔서 병이 들었다.

(4) 그녀는 게으름 때문에 실패했다.

(5) 그녀는 암으로 죽었다.

(6) 그는 찬비와 바람 때문에 감기에 걸렸다.

(7) 그는 의사를 부르러 보냈다.

(8) 나의 아버지는 작년에 여행을 했다.

(9) 버터는 우유로 만들어진다.

(10) 그녀는 서울 출신이다.

(11) 커피 좀 드시겠어요?

(12) 너는 아이들을 돌보아야 한다.

(13) 그녀는 자기의 할머니의 시중들기를 좋아한다.

(14) 나를 놀려대지 마라.

(15) 나는 도둑이었던 것을 부끄럽게 여긴다.

2. 다음 문장을 영작하시오.

(1) Where are you from?

(2) Wine is made from grapes.

(3) She is proud of her son's being a doctor.

(4) You have to get off at the next bus stop.

(5) I am tired with walking for a long time.

3. 다음 (   ) 안에서 알맞은 말을 고르시오.

(1) at, in   (2) till

(3) by   (4) for

(5) since   (6) to

(7) till   (8) since

(9) among   (10) across

(11) through   (12) along

(13) round   (14) around
(15) about   (16) of
(17) from   (18) with
(19) by   (20) from
(21) of   (22) into
(23) on   (24) at
(25) of   (26) from
(27) with   (28) of
(29) at   (30) up

4. 다음 (　) 안에 알맞은 말을 써 넣으시오.

(1) to   (2) which
(3) of   (4) in
(5) of   (6) by
(7) for   (8) at
(9) at   (10) at
(11) off   (12) of
(13) for   (14) on
(15) off

5. 다음 문장에서 잘못된 곳이 있으면 바르게 고치시오.

(1) pick up it → pick it up
(2) to see → to seeing
(3) during → for
(4) to → till
(5) at → on

6. 다음 영문을 우리말로 옮기시오.

(1) 언덕 위에 있는 그 집은 나의 것이다.
(2) 언덕 위에 아름다운 집이 있다.
(3) 당신은 다음 버스 정류장에서 내리는 것이 좋겠다.
(4) 나는 항상 그의 집 앞에서 버스를 탄다.

STEP BY STEP

가장 쉽게 배우는 강의식 기초 중학 종합 영어

중학영어

기초가
정답이다

독해 · 문법 · 회화 · 영작
스타트 기초 완성

방정인 저

반석출판사
Bansok

가장 쉽게 배우는 강의식 기초 중학 종합 영어

중학영어 기초가 정답이다

방정인 저 | 188*258mm | 252쪽 | 12,000원

30일 만에 끝내는
필수 영단어 3000여 개 수록

중학 매일 영단어 완전정복

Max Lee 편저 | 128*188mm |
496쪽 | 10,000원(mp3 파일 무료 제공)

30일 만에 끝내는
필수 영숙어 900개 수록

중학 매일 영숙어 완전정복

Max Lee 편저 | 128*188mm |
464쪽 | 10,000원(mp3 파일 무료 제공)